THE ULTIMATE REVOLUTION

THE ULTIMATE
REVOLUTION

Walter Starcke

HARPER & ROW, PUBLISHERS   *1817*

New York, Evanston, and London

THE ULTIMATE REVOLUTION. Copyright © 1969 by Walter Starcke. Printed in the United States of America. All rights reserved. No part of this book may be used or reproduced in any manner whatsoever without written permission except in the case of brief quotations embodied in critical articles and reviews. For information address Harper & Row, Publishers, Incorporated, 49 East 33rd Street, New York, N.Y. 10016. Published simultaneously in Canada by Fitzhenry & Whiteside Limited, Toronto.

FIRST EDITION

LIBRARY OF CONGRESS CATALOG CARD NUMBER: 73-85058

Contents

THE ULTIMATE REVOLUTION

Author's Note

The silence is broken. After centuries of loneliness and fear we are starting to listen to one another. Perhaps in our homes we are being pushed into listening by our young people because many of them are experimenting with dandies from the medicine cabinets powerful enough to transform them into strangers overnight. Perhaps in our cities we are being pushed into listening because of minorities that may set the streets afire in order to be heard. Perhaps internationally we are being pushed into listening because nations are playing with toys that can blow the whole world to bits if we don't listen to one other. Listening is no longer a luxury, it's a necessity. We may have been scared into communicating, but I, for one, am nevertheless delighted that it is finally happening.

All of us, old and young, black and white and yellow and red, saint and sinner, are individual persons trying to be heard.

I myself, in my listening, have come to realize that every person I have ever encountered, from grocery clerk to clergyman, from the stranger I casually passed in a crowd to my most intimate companion, has helped me to grow into whatever I am today. Each of us affects the other. Because you are what you are, I am what I am, and because I am what I am, you are what you are. For that reason I can say that I am not writing this book—you are, or rather everyone who has ever lived has contributed to it. We are all writing it. So let's see what we have to say to each other.

WALTER STARCKE

Introduction

Not long ago, I had a personal confrontation of agonizing proportions. I was out on the West Coast lecturing. For quite a while I had felt a pressure building up, a sense of frustration by trying to reconcile my naturally affirmative attitude toward life with a growing realization that revolution was part and parcel of today. Like many others, I tried to turn my eyes away from signs of revolution, I wanted to push out negative or disruptive images, but it was becoming increasingly difficult.

One day a particularly full schedule of appointments brought me in contact with a wide variety of people. I heard all manner of problems, bitternesses, and complaints from both those who were part of the so-called establishment and those who had left conventional life. I listened to people who were just plain paranoid, projecting their fears out onto everyone and everything they could. I listened to those who were on the side of the angels but who had also got caught up in fighting evil or projecting their fears onto society. I was struggling to keep my head above the onslaught of defeatism and lack of confidence or self-love I saw people express. To top it all off, every headline seemed to scream hate and violence. The noise of our music, the look of our clothes, and the smell of our air reflected one thing: revolution. There was no escaping it.

When I got back to my hotel I locked myself in and started to meditate, listen, think, and call on every spiritual and intellectual truth I knew in order to clear my own confusion. As the young say, I was working hard trying to pull my head together. I had to. The chips were down. My belief in God was on the block.

A long time ago I had come to the conviction that I wasn't alive without a sense of God—a universal divine purpose behind life, some transcendental oneness. I knew that I needed a kind of infinite beingness with which to relate in order to understand my own finite nature. I knew that anything worthy of being called God would have to be all-knowing, in all things, and all-powerful. So I had come to the conclusion that evil couldn't actually exist because we couldn't have God plus evil. If evil did exist, it had to be part of God, for God is everywhere and the only power. I found that when I was strong enough to look at evil without fear and see what was behind it I found out either that what appeared to be evil had a creative purpose or that it dissolved before my eyes as though I were waking from a bad dream.

It became apparent to me that those who were busily fighting evil or sin had a concept of God different from mine. At least, if they were claiming that God was omnipresent, omniscient, and omnipotent they were performing some fancy spiritual footwork in justifying those beliefs while at the same time resisting evil or sin.

That night in California I reminded myself of my beliefs. Then I measured the disturbing conditions I was seeing in the world against those principles. At last the light broke and I got my head and spirit clear. What I saw was alarming at first. I saw a nation staggering under a loss of faith. The American dream had been built on our positive attitude, our self-confidence, our belief in our infallibility, our ability to overcome obstacles, our sense of justice, and our belief in God. Now everywhere faith was collapsing like a house of cards.

In the past it was forgivable at one time or another to lose faith in most things, but it was unthinkable to lose faith in the United States itself. Now, however, great numbers were losing faith in the country. The older generation was confused and often trying to force faith on the young, but even the old timers' protestations of faith sounded as hollow as the forced flag-waving demonstration at a political convention. Finally it occurred to me what was behind this apparent loss of faith, and I could breathe again.

This tide of national, if not universal, loss of faith is good. It represents change. Whenever change takes place, faith in the old gives way to faith in the new, in things more worthy of faith. Man once had faith that the world was flat, but when he found out it was round he lost faith in his flat world. Scientists tell us daily of discoveries that make old systems obsolete, causing us to lose faith in the old ways. Evolution, revolution, change. They are all part and parcel of the same thing, and we will probably continue this process of gaining and losing faith over and over until we grow into our full spiritual being.

I realized then that I was wrong in fearing revolution. Any desire I might have had to turn the clock back to the "good old days" came because I was frightened by change. I didn't want to retreat to the past; I wanted to get *away from* the present. I wanted to drop out. When I pictured revolutionaries only as characters off the television screen angrily rushing around tossing Molotov cocktails and spitting obscenities, I was missing the point. Anyone who is dedicated to faith in the future of man, anyone who is willing to change and grow, is a revolutionary.

The tricky thing about growth is that it always assumes the appearance of an act of destruction. If I build a house I have to cut down some trees to make lumber. If I have a root-bound garden it becomes necessary to dig up all the plants, fertilize, and reset them in order for the garden to grow to greater glory. Someone who walks in just when I have ripped up all the plants is bound to be alarmed unless he has faith in the future.

Then it came to me: right now the world is being dug up. All the separate little patches of self-interest, all the unrelated hodge-podge of confusion, will, when the revolution is over, be assembled in one grand master plan resulting in a world more beautiful than I can imagine. All the hopes and dreams I have ever wanted for man, all the beautiful potential in the world, are ready to be fulfilled. I realized that the fulfillment of this potential was what the revolution was really about.

In the meantime I had to tell myself not to be confused by the signs of violence and disruption. Instead of panicking I had to have enough faith to look right at the disturbances to see what they could tell me. I saw that behind each disturbing sign was the crumbling of a system that had tricked man into putting his faith in a host of such unworthy objects as money, guns, and pills.

I looked at money. The financial revolution appeared in the form of an international monetary upheaval as nations politically manipulated currency. At home, taxes, insurance rates, and inflation made it increasingly impossible to hang on to personal wealth, thus forcing us to stop depending on money. I was amused to discover that in some of our poverty programs our government now finds it is cheaper to give money away without checking on the validity of the individual claims than to finance the mountain of paperwork necessary for verifying claims. Trust is now becoming an economic necessity. That's revolution.

When I looked at the disturbing signs of war, I realized that man had always put his trust in guns to get him what he wanted. But now the guns in our soldiers' hands are becoming obsolete not because of more efficient weapons but because of the power of the will within people. Numerically smaller countries now manage to stand against much larger and better-armed forces because of the will of the people for self-determination. At last right is becoming more powerful than might, and man will put his faith in right rather than in guns. That's revolution.

I looked at the disturbing reports that more of our hospital beds were filled with mental patients than with people suffering physical problems. Many of the nervous breakdowns were experienced by housewives and mothers who had placed their reliance on pills to keep them slimmed down and pepped up at the same time. Their pill prisons had alienated them from their own children and themselves. If it took a nervous breakdown to straighten out their false values and to teach them to place their faith in themselves it was worth the price.

I looked at people who were pained to see their churches empty, doors locked, to see their clubs unable to recruit new members, to see their governments unable to govern. Then it dawned on me that many of the systems were folding up because they had accomplished their purpose.

For instance, I heard complaints from those who were still trying to hang on to the old concept of church responsibility. They felt that the social welfare aims of their church in foreign and domestic fields were losing ground because the Peace Corps and government welfare programs were doing the job so much better. They didn't realize that the church's failure was a sign of its success. For many years the church was the only body interested in the social welfare of backward nations and the underprivileged in our own nation. But finally the church has succeeded in breeding man's basic human responsibility to his fellow man into our national conscience, into our government. Now the government with its enormous resources is doing the job. When the church leads the way in finding new and better systems, it is alive. Perhaps sometimes it has had to be emptied out in order to be filled up with fresh air. That's revolution.

The game of finding God behind disturbing appearances went on and on. Sometimes it took a long time for me to "let go" of my old beliefs in order to find new ones. The hardest belief to let go of was the belief in *good*. It's much easier to stop seeing bad, it's much easier to convince myself that I am being tricked by negative appearances, that something isn't really bad, than it is to get over believing things are good. But I found out that I couldn't reconcile bad appearances with a God of one power until I went beyond both bad and good, until I forced myself to look at things without any opinion whatsoever. Every time I managed to reach that judgeless stage beyond good and evil, I found freedom and with it a growing excitement about the adventure of life.

Finally I turned my attention to the student revolt. It seemed to me that the student revolution combined all aspects of the overall revolution. It was the very symbol of revolution. Most of us instinctively want to have faith in the young. Our hopes have to be pinned on the young: both their successes and their failures come to roost at our doorstep, for they are the product of the society we have fashioned in the past. Maybe that is why the older people get so upset when the young rebel. Then I realized that the young are bent on bringing into reality the world we taught them it was possible to have. They actually believe the American dream we talk about, only they see no reason why it can't be a world dream for everyone, no matter what sex or color. They may not always use the right means to achieve their ends, but the ends they seek are noble. These young people are our greatest successes. They are going to do what we dreamed of but failed to believe was really possible.

It came to me that the student revolt was hard to understand because students were revolting over something much deeper than easily understandable surface issues. They were fighting mainly to avoid being integrated into a society dominated by economic interests, a world whose techniques of brainwashing manipulated man, caused him to lose his sense of personal importance, and reduced him in turn to a grasping power-hungry machine contributing more to perpetuating old systems than to the development of his individual self. That was the key I was looking for—the importance of the individual.

Behind every aspect of the overall revolution there seem to be men who are waking up to an awareness of their personal self and its importance. When Malcolm X taught black people that they had been brainwashed out of realizing their true identity, he was speaking for all mankind, not just the black. Whatever our color, sex, nationality, size, or shape, we are *all* ignorant of our true identity and capacity, all faced with the problem of finding out who we really are. Perhaps this problem will go on and on until we wake up to our own godhood, to the actual fact that every single one of us is, as Paul said, "heir and joint heir with Christ in God"—not inferior to, not less than, but equal with, by nature of our oneness.

Everyone who refuses to give up his individual identity, who refuses to live in the service of any system which subordinates him, who refuses to be integrated into existing systems that lose sight of the importance of the individual, is a revolutionary proclaiming that the very foundation of our society is on trial.

I almost exploded when I realized how really wonderful that was. Always in the past we have busied ourselves putting salve on the individual sores of humanity. No sooner have we cured one trouble spot than another one has popped up. All the different signs of disruption and revolution were like individual sores on the body of mankind. We could go on forever fighting battle after battle, but if we want to put an end to sickness itself we sooner or later have to cure the bloodstream. We have to get at the underlying cause. All the individual revolutions we are witnessing on the campuses, in the streets, in the laboratories, in every conceivable area of life, add up to one thing. Man is now refusing to live any longer by laws that dehumanize him. MAN IS COMING OF AGE. Man is finding out who he is, and he's wonderful to behold. He sees no reason to continue putting up with sickness. He's going to rebel and rebel until the cause of revolution is eliminated.

The next thing I asked myself was: Then what law dehumanizes man? What single law has most brainwashed man? Right away it came to me how often I have heard people say, "Well, that's human nature," in order to excuse man's injustices and shortcomings. They say that the first law of human nature is survival, that man will always end up protecting himself at everyone else's expense, that human nature is selfish, treacherous, and evil. That's the lie this revolution is out to expose. In a crowded world we no longer have space for the selfish interests of what we have been taught to believe was human nature. The revolution will go on until that law is broken. The funny thing is that the mystics have told us for years and years and years that we had to overcome the first law of human nature, but only now are we being forced into it.

Why now? was my next thought. Long ago I was convinced that everything appearing on earth was at its level of being as a process of evolution. Man has taken countless centuries evolving into whatever he is today, and each stage was necessary for him. Mainly, he has been evolving out of his animal background into his humanity. Up to and including the present, he has been caught in the middle of the conflict between his animal instinct and his awakening spiritual instinct. As a matter of fact, he is body, mind, and spirit; so all three aspects have been evolving, but perhaps the body aspect has developed in advance of man's mental and spiritual evolvement. At any rate, most of what we have called human nature has actually been the remains of animal nature from which man has not yet fully evolved. The problem hasn't been with "human nature." It is that man's nature is just now becoming *fully human.* Man will now shake off the yoke of the old law of human nature, for he's evolved into his humanity. Whenever I see man acting out of fear, injustice, or cruelty, I can remind myself not to blame human nature. Instead I can think: Oh, he's still operating out of his subhuman nature.

When I came to the realization that mankind in general was just now coming into the fullness of humanity some other very important pieces fell into place. During my life I have gone through the whole range of rejecting religion, then finding ways to reconcile it with my life; rejecting Jesus Christ, then finding what a remarkable light he was and what incredible secrets were hidden in his message. I realized that because mankind is the product of evolution there had to be some one man who marked the advent of the first fully human being. If so, Jesus would represent that advent to the Western world and Buddha would to the East. No wonder the world instinctively worshiped these men. People knew Jesus and Buddha represented something profound that would be inherited by the whole of mankind. In fact, they said, "Greater works will ye do." No wonder they were considered revolutionaries. But more important, when I realized what these men represented in evolution and how mankind is beginning to catch up with their stage of evolution, I knew that it applied to me as well as others, that perhaps I too was growing into my Christhood or Buddhahood.

By this time, as you can see, I was ready to fly. I was ready to run up and down the streets shouting, "Ring the bells! Throw confetti from the rooftops! Deck the city with flags! Cover one another with flowers! Clap your hands and shout with joy, 'The revolution is here.' "

There was a practical down-to-earth reason for my joy. I found that by coming to this awareness I was able to reconcile a great number of things in such a way as to make it possible for me to love. No longer did I have to put anything down. I had always rather blamed man for his past shortcomings. I had blamed organizations and governments for their narrow-minded actions of the past. I had blamed a great number of people and things. Now I was released from judging the whole past history of man, for I saw that all the people and all the institutions of every period represented the stage of evolution the world was at. Perhaps the institutions would be wrong and harmful if they existed today, but they were the right ones for their time. I can't say the religions, governments, and laws of the past were wrong; they helped grow man into what he is today.

I could conceive that man is misguided when he tries to hang on to the old organizations or establishments of the past after he has actually evolved beyond them. When establishment's time is passed, it will strangle itself. Rather than resist or condemn establishment it seemed more devastating to build new and better ones. New establishments can be built now without the violence and subhuman means of the past, for now man has an awareness of himself and his humanity which he didn't in the past.

I saw that the revolution will now accomplish what it hasn't in the past because man's arrival at this stage of being fully human marks the most significant moment in the whole evolutionary process. Stages of evolutionary process have been marked from the beginning of time by the advent of different life forms. At each stage one life form has been dominant on earth, more developed and powerful than any other. After a time, a new form emerged as master, and on and on up until the present. For the past many thousand years subhuman paranoid man has dominated the earth, but now we are at the turning point. Man who views himself as a distinctly physical being, obsessed by fear—fear of hunger, fear of attack by his own kind, fear of loneliness, and a host of other fears —will no longer be in control.

Of course, fear-filled man as we know him will not disappear like the magician's rabbit. Probably for centuries there will be people living by the old limits of mind and nature, but they won't control the world as they have until this minute.

It seems to me that the man whom evolution is passing by is the fear-filled man gripped with paranoia. What most people have called man's human nature has really been his paranoid nature. What they have called the first law of human nature has actually been the first law of paranoid nature. Any time man projects his fears outside of himself onto other persons, places, governments, and things, then lets those fears motivate him, he is operating out of paranoia. Any time man has a persecution complex which makes him believe that others are out to harm him, any time he has a delusion of grandeur which makes him feel he is mentally, physically, or spiritually superior to others, any time he acts out of sexual frustration stemming from a doubt of his own virility, he is operating out of paranoia.

Without blaming anything from the past, I could see that a great deal of our society was built on paranoia, and in turn helped perpetuate it. Take law, for instance. I saw that all man-made law had to have a bit of paranoia in it because all laws were designed to resist some evil. Even the laws of art were designed to prevent faulty construction, to keep one from making a mess. As all establishment comes into being because of the laws defining it, all establishment has to possess a degree of paranoia. In the future we can learn to use laws to instruct man but not to resist evil, and we can have establishment which is constituted in such a way that it doesn't give rise to paranoia. I believe paranoia is going.

I can see proof of the departure of paranoia in our young people. So many of the young I have come to know take paranoia out in the open and look right at it. They have an amazing ability to smell out dishonesty. They won't brush it under the rug or let themselves be poisoned by it just because dishonesty is built into a system or is unintentional. The young refuse to live with paranoia. They refuse to put down natural man. They know that fear and evil are not natural states of man but rather are his conditions when he is not acting out of his full humanity. The young demand that life and man present wholeness.

This revolution to end paranoia is an actual end of life as we have known it. This is Armageddon.

I almost want to laugh when I write that. For so many years I have heard weird prophets trumpeting the end of the earth. Now all of a sudden I know they are quite right. Perhaps the end isn't the kind of end they envisioned, but it is just as dramatic and all-inclusive. I believe our way of life will soon change as drastically as it did when man came down out of the trees and began to civilize. With the disappearance of paranoia will go all the nations, organizations, systems, practices, teachings, and forms which perpetuate selfishness and fear, which divide up wealth and separate man from man. When that day comes, we will live as one big happy family. Hallelujah!

Off with Their Heads!

After I had arrived at my exalted conception of the ultimate revolution, I marched triumphantly into life, expecting to see the kingdom of heaven in full bloom. You can imagine what happened. Like Don Quixote I charged full steam into solid walls which didn't seem to understand they were supposed to dissolve before my love. With my paranoia-free vision aimed ever upward, I tripped over so many personal problems that I didn't know whether I was standing up or lying down. I found that banquets of pie in the sky didn't fill my stomach. So I limped back to the drawing board for another look.

When I took another look, I found my basic ideas checked out all right. I decided that I needed to discover some missing links in order for the chain of my conclusions to connect the old and the new. I felt that in this I wasn't alone. It seemed to me that a great number of those who had faith in the goals of the revolution were going about achieving them the wrong way by being somehow tricked into resorting to the same methods they wanted to do away with.

I usually try to solve a problem by getting back to the cause behind the cause behind the cause; so I started by looking at the surface injustices to which I was opposed. It was apparent that they were all brought on by man. Then I asked: What causes man to act out of his subhuman nature instead of his full capacity? In a world brimming with food, why does man not use his brain to get food to the right place at the right time? What makes man act with cruelty and lack of love to his brother? His instinct? No. He needs to have a brain even to follow his instincts. Then I realized: at the root of all of man's troubles is the improper use of his thinking capacity, his mind.

Well, bless its little heart. I had been so aware and proud of my mind—that part of me which reasons, calculates, rationalizes, and collects knowledge—that I hadn't realized it has been busily churning away creating a mixed bag of blessings and mistakes. I had thanked it for its blessings but had gone out fighting other people, believing them responsible for errors that really lay at the doorstep of my own mind. I should have realized a long time ago what a hassle my mind has given me. So many times I saw the world as a dark and miserable place, only to view it as a rosy heaven the next minute. What had actually changed? Nothing except the interpretation my mind had put on things. At least I knew that before I could point my finger at others I should understand my own mind and get it pulled together.

I couldn't blame my poor mind though. Whenever I forgot my connection with life, when I lost sight of my true identity, when I lost my God contact, my mind had to run my life for me. The dear thing rushed around doing the best it could, but it needed help from the rest of me. When I let my mind run things by itself, it was as though I were trying to operate a car on a third of its cylinders. In the new day man will live with his whole self—body, mind, and spirit. So I realized that if I am to live fully, I have to understand how the mind works and what its purpose is.

It seems to me that my mind should be an instrument designed for my use, not vice versa. All too often it has run me as though I were its servant. It has kept me awake when it wished, it has made me heavy with gloom at times, it has made me hate, but it has also helped me create, it has helped me translate awareness into action, and to communicate, and it has even helped me experience God. Obviously the mind is a necessary instrument, and those teachings or religions that advocate hitting it over the head with a mental hammer or blotting it out have missed the point. The mind is like a chisel in the hands of a sculptor. The sculptor needs a chisel to work with. He can't claw the stone with his fingernails. To become a master he must take good care of his chisel, keep it clean, sharp, and in good shape, but he has learned not to let the chisel run his life for him.

So in order to understand my mind I turned once more to evolution. It seemed to me that in the process of evolution, the development that separated man from the other animals was the evolvement of man's reasoning faculty. If there were some kind of chart indicating the different stages of development of life on earth, it would show a phase representing human existence. This phase would start with the advent of the reasoning faculty and would end with the final full development and control of the mind. All in between would be the various stages of man's battle to gain control of his mind and to discipline it. Maybe that's what the revolution is really about, the final control of the mind. After all, man's mind has now grown so strong it has created a scientific technology capable of turning the world into paradise. The only thing that stands in the way is the misuse of that same mind. When the misuse is eliminated, the human phase will be completed. Perhaps that time is now.

At any rate, I can't blame the mind for not coming into being fully developed or for starting out as such a mess. Most new creations start out unrefined and must be worked on and developed into a finished product.

Our minds are like computers. The mind operates on the information that is fed into it. If the information is bad, the answers that come out of the computer are false. If the information is honest, the computer can bring forth wonderful results. It, in itself, is neither bad nor good. But when a computer is programmed with monstrous paranoid information, its results are monstrous. Unfortunately, at present the world mind is working on much too much paranoid information and producing like results.

But even here, man or the mind is not to blame. Right at the beginning, the mind was fed some inadequate information, and it has been acting on it ever since. Most animals live by the testament of the senses. Man evolved out of animal life; so naturally the first information fed to his computerlike mind was information from the senses. He took what he saw, touched, tasted, smelled, and heard to be the truth and acted on it. But the senses were highly inadequate authorities, and their information was far from accurate. Because the information was a lie, man's actions were based on fear. Fear fueled further fear, self-perpetuating misinformation, so that man has never known what it is to be free. That is, except for a few who have managed freedom, man has never known what it is to have a mind completely programmed with truth.

Many of the young consciously or unconsciously want to shake their computers loose from the misinformation or limitations fed to them by the senses. That's why they have been trying to expand the senses. They have blasted the ears with sounds out of the normal hearing range, they have blasted the eyes with visually disturbing color vibrations, and some of them have blasted all their perception with sense-exploding drugs. Many of the young also have the capacity to believe in invisibles, which frees them from depending solely on sensual information.

When I realized that my mind had to be cleared of the misinformation with which it was programmed—cleared of the brainwashing—and when I realized that I had to then learn how to program the mind with data which would make it operate out of love rather than fear, I knew what it meant to be a real revolutionary. I saw that my first responsibility if I wanted to bring about the new day was to take care of my own head. I decided that the next time I charged out into the world I would have my head in shape even if I had to take it off to work on it.

This realization set off a chain of thoughts. Perhaps the French revolutionaries were not far wrong when they said, "Off with their heads!" The present revolution seems to be symbolized by a statement which is just as revealing: "Blow your mind!" A great number of people today have been deliberately blowing their minds with drugs because they have come to realize that their own mind was at the root of their problem. Many have become aware that their minds have been brainwashed with information hypnotizing them with false values, fear, and a sense of inequality; so they have tried to use drugs to jar their minds loose. Others have trooped to psychiatrists, hoping to get their minds wrung out.

It seems obvious to me that we can pass all the laws in the world prohibiting the use of drugs, but it won't make any difference. Until we find spiritual ways to clear the mind of its subhuman information, people will use any material help they can get despite possible dangers. At last man is aware that the only thing standing between him and freedom is his own head.

Suddenly I realized why those who are trying to blow their minds in one way or another are called "heads." They know they are playing with their heads. Some have even got so carried away that they are practically making toys out of their heads as they experiment with every possible drug to see what different effects each has on the mind. Somehow they have caught the vision that their minds are only a part of their equipment of self, not their whole selves, and they want to understand that part as well as keep it from fooling them into believing it is the whole show.

The so-called "head" language has spread into most of the young world and it tells the story. In the past man confused his self with his mind, so when someone asked, "How are you?" he would answer, "I'm depressed," or "I'm happy," revealing that he thought his self inseparable from the condition of his mind. Today we hear, "How's your head, man?" And if the person is low, his answer is, "I'm in a bad head." Both today's question and today's answer reveal no confusion of the mind with the larger self. A person can admit to having a mind or "head" and that it can make him low or high, but he doesn't have to think that the mind is the self.

Once more I checked these thoughts out by seeing how they fit the two greatest heros of the revolution, the first fully developed men, Jesus and Buddha. They were really head-masters. They both told us to work on our heads. Both of them appeared to be advocating the overthrow of the governments and systems which enslaved mankind, but actually neither of them advocated the use of violence, neither of them advocated fighting the enemy on the outside or resisting outside evils. They told us that the enemy is our own mind when it is filled with judgment and fear.

Yet, Jesus and Buddha were not impractical saints gently walking around the country asking people to drop out. Their lives were no picnic. Buddha had to rip up all his roots, leave his family, and turn his back on money and power because of his realization that he had been duped by his mind into an illusory sense of self and he knew he had to find a way to freedom.

Jesus advised us, "The birds of the air have nests, the animals have holes, but the son of man (the revolutionary) has no place to lay his *head,*"and "Take no *thought* for the morrow, what ye shall eat and what ye shall wear." Jesus really insulted the rational mind. The mind couldn't help but balk at his statement, "If somebody sues you for your coat give him also your cloak." It makes no rational sense. The mind would have to say: "You idiot, if you give away both your coat and your cloak, there's nothing to keep you warm. You'll freeze." It isn't logical.

That seems to bring it down to the real crux of the matter. This is a revolution to reveal the whole man. It won't be won by logic alone. It won't be won by anything alone. Faith without action won't succeed, action without logic won't succeed, and logic without faith won't succeed.

I could no longer kid myself. Whenever I find logical reasons for violence, condemnation, and hate, no matter which side I am on, I am selling out the real revolution. I may have temporary mental or physical victory, but I will mess up my head by neglecting my spirit and I will lose myself. I cannot put the blame outside my self. I can't say others or establishment have brainwashed me—I have really done it to myself. I cannot say I have faith in anything if I take action not based on faith.

So now I am back to my starting point in this introduction—how to reconcile faith with my human problems. I see that my logical mind, which has tricked me into all kinds of self-defeating actions, has an Achilles' heel by which it is going to be put into its place without my having to fight it.

The logical mind has grown so strong that it is finally exposing its own limitations. It equates faith with perfection and absolutes, but there are no absolutes at the finite level. The mind says that I must lose faith whenever I find imperfections in a thing or system; however, now the mind has grown so sharp that it exposes flaws in everything, including itself. Perfection at the material level is relative. If I make a million similar objects, a microscope will show me that no two are exactly alike. So which one is perfect? None. Perfection is relative. I will never find perfection at the finite level. Whenever I am tricked by logic to believe I can find any perfect person, place, or thing, I am bound to end in failure.

When I lose faith in law, I find faith in man. When I lose faith in man, I find faith in the source of that man, just as all of Jesus' disciples had to lose faith in him in order to find it in themselves. When I lose faith in my own self, I become free of the brainwashing which told me I was a limited finite man, and I find faith in God. When I lose faith in God, I find that I have had faith in a too narrow concept of God. I find that the God I had faith in was a paranoid concept of God. I was using it as a weapon I could employ to overcome my enemies, as a policeman to keep life in line, as something apart from myself, off in heaven. When I lose faith in that God, I find God is really within me, is me.

Then what can I humanly do? A saying of Jesus' pops into my head: "Judge righteous judgment." Don't judge by appearances; don't judge in terms of a logical mind that puts things down by saying, "That's bad," or "That's good."

When I look out at the world with my senses colored by judgment, it is as though I am looking at a scene through a pair of cracked colored glasses. The scene is there. I can identify houses, trees, and people. But as long as I have the glasses on, those objects are all flattened out, the colors are gone, cracks run through everything. However, if I take the glasses of judgment off, if I have enough love to see without falling for good and evil, the world is there in all its glory. It is entirely different from the one seen through the glasses. Things have the same shape; I see houses, trees, and people; but now they are not distorted. Perhaps this is what the mystics meant when they said the world was illusion. The world seen through cracked colored glass is illusion.

Now I know what Jesus meant when he said, "My kingdom is not of this world." He wasn't putting the earth down. The whole secret of his message is that the kingdom of heaven is right here at the material level if I can only "see" it. He meant that his kingdom was not of the world dominated by subhuman nature. "This world" stood for the world of paranoia. He meant that when we put an end to paranoia his kingdom will appear right here on earth where it belongs.

I see that the secret of untangling the confusion of life lies in understanding what the mystics call the third and fourth dimensions of life. They say that everything one can recognize at the phenomenal level, the everyday down-to-earth level of life, is the third dimension. Anything that can be named, labeled, or thought about is third-dimensional. The fourth dimension is the spiritual dimension, the total, the infinite. At the fourth dimension everything is comprehended in its pure beingness, in its oneness and unity. The catch is that thinking is limited to the third dimension. The fourth dimension, like God, is something that can be experienced but not thought about, for thought always limits. The two levels are present simultaneously but not really understandable in terms of each other. Since they are two different senses, one can't understand the fourth dimension in terms of thought any more than a blind man can comprehend color.

When Jesus talked about his kingdom he was referring to the fourth dimension of life. Someday man will live in the fourth dimension as though he were seeing without the colored glasses of judgment. In the meantime we are both the man of earth, operating out of our finite sense of self, and the man of God, one with the whole of life.

My problem had been that I had got the two confused. A spiritual instinct sensed the reality of the fourth dimension, but my mind tried to find it at the third dimension. God existed at the fourth dimension, but I kept looking to see God with my third-dimensional understanding. I kept trying to see God in war, in government, in establishment, but these things are part of my man of earth self. I kept trying to bring God down to this level, when the only way God can be experienced is to take this level up to God by refusing to judge it in terms of bad and good. Then oneness can be experienced. When the fourth dimension is experienced, a transition comes about. We are lifted to a higher vibration or sense of truth, and miraculously, when we are once more at the third dimension we find a kind of healing or improvement has taken place. It's even possible to become so in tune with this dimension that we can say as Paul did, "I live but not I"—though he was operating at the third dimension his fourth-dimensional sense of the allness was directing him.

That is what Jesus meant when he said, "I and my father are one, but my father is greater than I." He was saying: My third and fourth dimensions are one, but the fourth dimension is the greater. He wasn't talking about duality or separation. He wasn't going back to a belief in a God off somewhere. He meant that the inner man can manifest itself as the outer man.

It seems to me that the purpose of our revolution against subhuman nature is to lead us into the fourth dimension, where we do not live by effects, where we do not "live by bread alone," or money, or guns, but where we live by virtue of our capacity to contact the infinite invisible, fully human, fourth dimension. The fourth-dimensional consciousness becomes ours, and our reliance, faith, and understanding are operated out of the oneness of life, not out of our trying to find a power to use over our enemies.

The attainment of this fourth-dimensional consciousness is what the mystics call illumination. It is the secret of harmonious living without strife, struggle, or paranoia. This freedom of illumination is really freedom from ignorance, for only ignorance holds us to the belief that life is dependent on things and people in the external sense. When we understand that our body, our mind, and our spirit belong to us and that we govern them, we become free. We are given a mind as a thinking apparatus so that we can think the thoughts we want to think as our man of earth self, but we can determine what we let occupy our mind. We are given a body, but we are not limited to that body except at the third dimension. We are given a spirit to keep our minds and bodies pure. With these three we can lift ourselves into the fourth-dimensional consciousness where life begins to flow more by grace than by effort, where the I of us embraces infinity, and good can then flow forth from our consciousness into the visible.

The Ultimate Revolution is my exploration into ways of living which can help make the bridge from the third-dimensional world to the fourth, into the paranoia-free world following revolution. It makes suggestions how to work with both our earth selves and our God selves. It explores how we can achieve greater unity with our selves and others through our actions and our sexual instincts, how we can use the material effects of the world for greater wholeness and how we can contact the source of spirit for guidance. It is a journey from the darkness of the third dimension to the illumination of the fourth dimension.

CHAPTER ONE

The Morality of Grace

Have you ever watched a sunrise? When you sit through the long night, expecting a new day, some kind of faith that the light will break has made the waiting possible. But even faith is challenged when the clock says the sun is due to rise in three or four short minutes and there isn't even a hint of light, as though some sort of cosmic betrayal has taken place. Maybe your clock has gone crazy. The dark is so deep that it is impossible to believe there will be light in just a matter of seconds. Then, just in the nick of time, there is a soft glow on the horizon, holding out a kind of pink promise for the day ahead.

When the light starts adding color to the world, the simplest objects begin to take on a sort of beauty and shriek out their right to be, that each of them has a purpose in life. You look at your own body, your own hands and feet, as though they are newly created wonders, and they too have a purpose. Everything has a purpose, and that mutual purpose welds you and all the world together into one beingness.

That's the kind of position those of us are in who have been waiting through the dark revolution for the sunrise of humanity. There is still a great deal of darkness around—in fact, it is darkest before the dawn—but the darkness has served its purpose. The world has slept. Now it's ready to wake up; it's ready to take on its true colors. Who can help but be excited at the wonderful things there will be to do now, full of light, no longer done in darkness? Everything has to be reseen in the light of day.

Most of us need a whole reeducation of "how" to live in the light of day. We are so used to groping around on our hands and knees in the dark that we have to learn how to stand up straight in our full humanness, experiencing life rather than just touching it with our fingers. That's what this moment, the one right at hand, is all about. The old world has been pretty well shook up by the revolution. The dust hasn't even settled yet. In fact, there is more to be kicked up before the day is fully here. The emerging is just beginning. There are pieces lying all over the place that need homing— need to be mentally and spiritually lined up with their true purpose and place. Some of us who consider ourselves revolutionaries had better start setting up guidelines for living in the light, or we will, as the old saying goes, win the war and lose the peace.

Perhaps we had better start by taking a look at ourselves. If everything has a place and a purpose, what's ours?

I personally have spent many years with a feeling that I was not in my right place and right time. I got along in the world, but I never felt quite at home. Now I realize that I *was* in my right place and in my right time, only the right time for the main purpose of my life just hadn't come yet. I'm a day person. My real job isn't tearing down but building up, and the day for building couldn't come until the revolution was over or at least nearing its end. Now I know that I can throw myself into life with the whole of my being, with the full sense of the rightness of the time and place—it's the reconstruction.

For that matter, I can see now that most of the people to whom I have felt drawn, most of my close friends, are also reconstructionists. Some of them have worked for years, wrestled with metaphysical truths, stumped their toes on spiritual enigmas, always feeling that out there must be a world where they could feel more at home. Others have worked hard, been conscientious in their zeal to live up to the highest truth possible, only to see others less qualified and less talented achieve greater success in the world. Most likely those of my friends whose success didn't measure up to their industry and talent were in that dilemma because they were people being prepared for their place in the world of reconstruction. Their day just hadn't come yet.

Well, it's here now, and with it we can all see that everything in the past and everybody we met on the way was necessary for our growing into what we are today, and for the living of this day. If we felt confusion because our philosophy or religion was unable to bring us the freedom it promised, perhaps it was because just as we were being grown, so was our religion or philosophy growing from the dark into the light.

Apart from those of us who have been on earth for enough time to have struggled through the long night, whole generations of the young were being born who were prepared from ages past for the job of being reconstructionists. These generations leave no doubt that their differences are not, as in the past, simply modifications of their parents' values; they are a whole new breed whose being is tuned to a different song. That song, though few have recognized its sound, is a love song. It's the music of the new, paranoia-free world, the world where the sound of the mind has given way to the song of the spirit.

From my association with many of these young, I think it would be pretty safe to say there is little doubt that their instinctive and easy understanding of the most mystical of truths qualifies them as children of light whose affinity for the reconstruction period isn't an accident. No wonder the young have been confused. They couldn't help but look at the world of paranoia and feel they had got there by mistake. They had the capacity for love, for reconstruction, but were set down on the earth while the revolution was in full swing. They wanted to love everything and everybody, they wanted to be happy, but they were told that happiness was something to be worked toward for the future, not experienced now. They rightly couldn't understand why there had to be a disparity between what they felt and the way they were supposed to act. While we talked about the spirit, they felt it, and those to come will *be* it.

The young don't have to be sold on the new day; they don't have to develop the sensitivities needed to live in the new day as do many of the older people; they don't have to "learn" how to love. They already "are." But they do need to understand what they feel; they need to be able to articulate what they feel. For that matter, all of us who want to be part of the light world, who want to throw ourselves fully into growing tomorrow, into building the earth, need some "hows," some guidelines. We are all in the same boat. We aren't young people, we aren't hippies, we aren't old people. Those classifications belong to the past; we are all one thing— reconstructionists.

We are all in the same boat for another reason: none of us can claim a nice pat set of rules on how to live in the new day. Each of us has something to contribute to the new way of life, but none of us has a complete answer. How could we? The new day is just dawning.

Perhaps the world is on the verge of a new religion to fit this new day, one that couldn't have evolved until the new day actually evolved. Perhaps each one of us will add something individually unique to make up the wholeness of this new religion. However, often in chemistry when different ingredients are mixed together, they not only lose their old qualities but result in a totally new substance. So though a new religion could be a curious blend of the old and the new, it may be totally new.

We shouldn't be surprised to have a new religion arrive at this time. After all, the world has been here millions of years yet conscious awareness became active only in the geologically recent past, and our commonly accepted realization of the importance of consciousness has come only during the past century with the advent of psychology and psychiatry. Yes, perhaps we are on the brink of a totally new religion which will not only encompass the whole man but will also encompass total awareness of all levels of life, total experience, total space, total time—the total universe.

A New Morality

Speculations on a new religion might be good material for new-day dreaming, but at this point we have a lot to do at a much less lofty pinnacle. As a matter of fact, if a new religion does evolve, it will come as a result of the new day and will be the creation of total mankind rather than the expression of any one person. In the new day the emphasis willl be taken off the individual *I* and will be placed on the *We I*, and all creations, even religions, will be seen as a product of the universal self of man. Paradox—that's not far off from what Jesus was trying to say, is it? So perhaps the totally new is totally old, but, being new to mankind in general, it is totally new.

At any rate, as an exploration into new territory, this book will be far from complete; it will rather hint at a direction. I will be the voice for this particular expedition, but we are all contributing to it. The suggestions I lay down will be drawn from contributions everyone has made to my consciousness. If it adds up to some kind of "feel" for where we are to go, if it can be reappraised and the routes retraveled until the waters of the new world are charted, it will have served a purpose. If these beginnings influence others to chart their own courses, we will have discovered and built tomorrow.

We all know plenty of abstract truth. We have volumes of metaphysical dissertation on the esoteric level of man's being, on his spiritual nature, on pure spiritual principle, and all of that can indeed be the source of our ideas, but if we don't get right down to specifics, down to *how* to live right now, it does no good.

"How to live" implies morality. It's hard to keep from shuddering at the word "morality." We associate it with the morality of the past, but we need some aids on how to live in the new day, and that is what a morality is. When things are all going well, when we are in contact with our center, when we are in our right place, nothing is needed; but anyone who dares to grow, who dares to be creative, isn't always in contact. When we are out of contact we need some guidelines to keep us on the track until we find ourselves again.

Existent morality was created during the dark period and doesn't fit the new day. It has obviously broken down. We either instinctively refuse to follow it, realizing the hypocrisy and superficiality, or we rather grudgingly go on giving it lip service because we know we need some kind of morality and can't imagine a new one.

The old morality was the morality of law. It was structured on law, on bad and good, because it was designed for man who lived under the domination of his mind. He needed laws because he couldn't recognize inner guidance. Because man couldn't realize in the dark that everything had its place and its use, he believed he had to protect his family; so he made laws condemning everything which he thought was out of place, everything he didn't understand. He couldn't trust himself to find what things were and where they belonged. Therefore, the old morality wasn't spiritual; it couldn't be. Laws are designed to resist evil, designed with a negative spirit behind them. Resistance is created by fear; it is not spirit-led.

To put it another way, the old morality applied to the third dimension, where man took the testimony of the senses and believed that life was limited to all the things he could identify with his mind, to the phenomenal sense of life. At that level, self-preservation was paramount and everything fell under the title of bad or good. Everything had to be one or the other.

The morality of law inhibits freedom because law can't change. If it is riddled with too many exceptions it ceases to be law. It has to apply to all people at all times, so it kills spontaneity in living. If we want to find a new morality we must find one which applies to each situation individually, allowing spontaneity in living. It is complicated because this kind of morality must constantly change, and those afraid of change can't free themselves to follow it.

Now, the old morality of law was right for its time. It was indeed the best way to cope with the dark world, and it is still best for those who haven't developed spiritual sight. But that which was right in the dark is insanity in the light. Actually, this is pointed out in the New Testament. Jesus said, in effect: We can't put down the laws of old; they serve their purpose at their own level, but the only way we can do away with all law is by living in grace—or love. You see, love has nothing to do with bad or good; love resists nothing; love is never negative. Love is not only spiritual or fourth-dimensional, it is the very fourth dimension itself.

Then how about calling our new morality—our morality of love, our fourth-dimensional morality—the Morality of Grace, to differentiate it from the old morality of law? Grace is a word connoting the action of love or the action of spirit; so, as a morality is nothing more than a collection of suggestions on how to act, a Morality of Grace would be suggestions or guidelines on how to live without violating the spirit of love. A Morality of Grace is only a collection of suggestions designed to aid those who know they *have* to live fourth-dimensionally, those who know they can't return to the dark or exist by the old morality.

Then how do we start formulating this Morality of Grace? The first and cardinal test we can make of any action or thought is to see if the suggested action has any implication of bad or good. Whenever we put something down as being either bad or good, we are under law, the laws of bad and good; we have implanted the seeds of a belief in a power apart from God, the existence of evil, a world less than whole. You might suspect that there is no way to avoid this, but I don't agree. It can be done. We can find ways to label moments of temporary light or dark without condemnation or judgment.

For instance, we have accepted the fact that nothing has been created for evil; only the use or rather the misuse can be destructive. Everything is *for* some thing or some place. We have no problem when things are in their right place, but we need a morality to help us face a thing which is not in its right place "for" doing what it is "for." So, when we see painful or disturbing signs, our first job, under a Morality of Grace, is to find out, or ask ourselves: What's that for? When we are faced with a person who troubles us, we can ask: What's he for? When we contemplate that which people and things are "for," we begin to see rightness in them, we are knowing the truth about them; and knowing is loving, so we are starting to love them.

As a matter of fact, we should always start with our own selves. Our number one responsibility is to keep ourselves in our own right place. So, whenever there is a disturbance or personal frustration, we should start by asking ourselves: Am I in my right place? Am I doing what I am "for"?

Now, this is not saying that we or everything else is at present in its right place, doing what it is "for." Far from it. The light is just beginning to show us the truth. We have been knocking things over in the dark for so long that the world is a veritable jigsaw puzzle of misplaced people and ideas. It may take us many years to put ourselves and other persons and things into their right places, but this is how we start.

When we see something that disturbs us, when we are tempted to return to the old judgments which trick us to say, "I'm bad," "I'm good," or "That's bad," "That's good," we can stop. We can really look at the situation or thing and try to imagine how it could be productive, how it could belong, how it could serve a purpose. We can keep looking, keep refusing to judge, until we find a possibly constructive purpose, because there is a purpose somewhere for everything. When we find it, we are free from condemning the situation. We can see that it appeared harmful or distasteful simply because it was out of place.

After we have found out what something is "for," we will either see that it is already doing its thing and therefore we have nothing to fear, or we can help put it in its true place so that it can fulfill itself in a constructive way. When we help guide something back into being what it is "for," the destructive or inharmonious aspects will disappear. This is done with no condemnation, no judgment, no resistance of evil, no trying to unsee or condemn something by claiming it doesn't exist—and incidentally, but most importantly, the disturbance is eliminated without our filling ourselves with the poison of self-condemnation or the poison we take on by condemning others. That's pure love for both our own self and others.

It seems almost too simple to say that knowing what we are "for" is an act of self-love, but what could be more loving than to know we are united with God or beingness? Rest assured, we are all where we should be at every moment when we realize that even our frustration is there to direct us toward fulfilling our reason "for" being in the world. Perhaps we can't always return either ourselves or others to their rightful place in a moment, but once we open our consciousness to try it, we are on the road. Don't forget, we are at the dawn of this new age, and when the light is fully here, the universal house will be in perfect order.

Grokking and Grooving

Let's take this business of knowing what something is "for" another step. In the past we considered we "knew" something when we simply understood it with our minds and could call it by its name, but we were not living as total beings. When we come into the fourth-dimensional life, we realize that "knowing" means not only the report of the senses and the rational mind but the actual experience as well. Knowing comes from a total involvement. In this sense, we don't know a work of art, a flower, a person, a mathematical formula, or any truth unless we not only behold it but to some extent experience and become it.

As long as man thinks of himself as a separate entity cut off from all other people and life, he can't possibly allow himself to experience many things wholly. His nervous system can't take it, or rather his feeling of security can't take it. As long as man thinks there is evil in the world, he can't allow himself to let go and indiscriminately experience life, because he might be crushed both by evils from without and by evils he finds within his own self. Many people have to learn how to experience. Reading about experiencing is one thing, but being free enough to open one's own self to it is another. Schools have even been set up now for the sole purpose of teaching people how to experience life. When man begins to ache to experience himself fully, he aches to experience everything and everyone around him.

Perhaps the single most difficult element for the older generation to understand in its attempt to know the young is the importance the young place on experiencing. If there is any generation gap, that is it. Older people have been conditioned in a world in which the experience of a person, place, or thing was not consciously included as part of knowing. If they saw something and understood it with their minds, they thought they knew it, whatever it was. But the young have come along, perhaps more highly evolved, and they just naturally feel that to know something is to see it, feel it, touch it, think it, and experience it—if not "be" it.

Both the young and the old are confused in their attempts to communicate with each other, for when they talk about knowing something, they think they are talking about the same thing, but they aren't. The young think the old people have experienced what they talk about, and the old can't understand that the young cannot and will not accept anything that they haven't experienced. The old are confused by some of the methods the young are using in their attempt to experience life wholly, and the young can't understand why the old don't appreciate the need to experience and expand.

Many of the young have experimented with drugs in order to satisfy their need to "know" or experience life more fully because there was no existing formalized morality which could help them do it in a natural way. Some older people sampled drugs themselves to try to find out why the young were turning to drugs, but they sat around waiting for drugs to give them the kind of kicks alcohol does and missed the point. The young were trying drugs in order to feel different dimensions and not just extensions of the old ones.

If we can come up with a Morality of Grace which helps us experience life more fully, it will fit both the young and the old. It will help the young to experience life as whole persons in a natural way, and it will help the older people stretch until they can experience new dimensions of themselves and a whole new life of total wonders. Since the fourth dimension must be experienced rather than thought, only a morality based on grace rather than law can lift us into it.

In forming our new morality, we can use some new words to help us. It's no accident that new words keep coming into our vocabulary via the young. New people are products of a new day, and they demand words to fit. At least, they are attracted to words which are not conditioned by old interpretations. The young condition their own words to fit the changes of consciousness.

One of these new words for which there is no adequate equivalent comes from the novel *Stranger in a Strange Land*, by Robert Heinlein, which has become a kind of classic among the young and hippie world. The word is a perfect word, and I don't know any other that quite fills the bill as it does. The word is "grok." It means the total knowledge and experience I was just talking about.

To grok something is to understand it from all levels: to see it, to comprehend it, to understand it both spiritually and physically, to experience it, to identify with it, and, above all, to discern what it is "for." The hero of Heinlein's story groks people as well as situations. He often retreats inside himself until he can fully grok a situation or person. Then he acts, but his actions are not based on partial information, not on bad or good, for he has achieved not only the experience of the person or situation but an awareness of the true place of that person or situation in the scheme of things.

Another new word, which has already reached enough acceptance to be listed in *The Random House Dictionary*, is "groove" or "groovy." To groove on something is to zero in on it, to focus on it fully, to concentrate on it and put oneself fully into comprehending it. In order to grok something, it is necessary to groove on it.

We groove on a person, place, thing, or situation with our whole attention in hopes that we will arrive at the place where we can see if it is in its right place, doing whatever it is for. If we succeed, we find that the person, place, thing, or situation is groovy.

"Groovy" is the adjective which describes successful grooving. When a person says, "Hey, that's groovy," he is saying that he has grokked the situation and sees how it fits in with the whole.

The word "groovy" doesn't fall under the onus of being a degree word of bad or good. Nothing is almost groovy. It is either groovy or not; it either has been grokked and is groovy or one hasn't grokked it yet and it isn't groovy. There aren't any set laws for what is groovy or isn't. What is groovy today may not be tomorrow, because tomorrow it may not be in its place doing what it is for.

Actually, the importance of grooving on life is not all that new, but our realization of its importance is new. Jesus gave us explicit instructions on why it is necessary to groove on both where we are and the moment we are in. He said, "The ground on which you stand is holy ground." You should groove on it. No matter where we are, no matter where we find ourselves, the very spot is holy ground if we really groove on it and grok it.

When we project ourselves into other places, when we spend time wishing we were somewhere else, we are denying that we are in our rightful place at that moment. Wanting to be somewhere else or in some other time is a put-down of where we are. Actually, if we really groove on the place at which we are, really get the most out of it and understand it, we will be free to go elsewhere. If we are not where we think we would like to be, it is probably because we have not grokked or loved the place we are in at the present.

A cardinal suggestion we can add to our Morality of Grace is to be sure we are grooving on our present "here." We can examine it, see what it has to show us, look around ourselves, understand the holy-ness of the ground on which we are standing. We can bring our whole selves, body, mind, and spirit, and open our eyes to the grooviness of the spot we are in. Believe me, it will love us in return.

The next suggestion we can add to our morality is grooving on the now. Jesus said, "Take no thought for the morrow.... Consider the lilies of the field . . ." and so on. How dare we waste the now or not appreciate it? We certainly will never have it again. At every moment we can ask ourselves: Am I fully grokking this very moment? Am I seeing it in all its fullness and richness? Am I cheating myself out of the appreciation of this very moment? Am I really experiencing this moment, or have I let my mind trick me off into thinking about the past or future? Look at this moment. How many levels am I open to?

As long as we are looking over the shoulder of life, grooving on neither the place nor the time, we have cut ourselves off and are loving neither ourselves nor life. Of course, it is more pleasant to groove on the highs, but unless we learn to groove on the lows as well, we are not grooving on the moment.

In the past, we just wanted to escape from lows as soon as possible, to get rid of them, and that was all. Now we see that we must grok the lows. They have their purpose. So when we have a low, let's not be cheated. Let's experience it. Look at it. See what it has to tell us. Probably when we have grokked it, we will never have to experience that kind of low again. It will have served its purpose.

It's tempting to take a tranquilizer or drug in order to avoid lows, but by tranquilizing ourselves out of the lows we have denied a gift of life. If we have tried to grok a low situation, tried to handle it with spirit, tried to lift it by reestablishing ourselves within and been unable to make the difficult time pass, it probably means that the low is trying to tell us something. If we turn off with a drug or drink, or any of the other outside dodges, such as sex for sex's sake, we may have simply pushed the low experience away from ourselves, and in the future we will have to go through the whole process all over again. We may have cheated ourselves of the lesson we could have learned. How much more fruitful and affirmative,

how much more loving of ourselves and of our lives it would have
been if we had grooved on the low until we had grokked it and
found out what it had for us.

Ups and Downs

Grooving on our lows is a lot like grooving on our mistakes.
Often we try to ignore our mistakes or faults, but that's like trying
to ignore a splinter. The sooner we groove on the splinter and see
how to get rid of it, the sooner we are free of the pain or annoyance
caused by the splinter.

Our mistakes are pretty much what the old morality referred to
as sins. The old morality kept fighting sin and condemning it.
When we didn't know to groove on sin, it grew into a monster. The
only way to get rid of sin is to embrace it, throw it kisses, see what
it has to say. Loving is knowing; so when we understand the purpose of sin we love it to death.

The problem we have in understanding our sins or our mistakes
is that they only exist at the third-dimensional level. The fact that
they exist there must mean that they are necessary at that level. If
we want a morality to help us arrive at the fourth dimension, we
need to redefine sin so that it can be freed of the condemnation of
the old morality.

In order not to judge or condemn in the old way, many people
today talk in terms of "ups" and "downs." Anything that lowers
them into a darker sense of life is called a down, and anything that
lifts them into the light is an up. Downs make people lose contact
with themselves. Anything that makes a person fall out of love with
himself is a down; it makes him fall out of love with God. You might
say any down which alienates the self from God is a sin.

Some people might say, "Well, the old sins alienated man from
God." That's true. I'm not putting down all the old laws. I am
simply saying that many of the old laws were based on fear instead
of love and therefore they were incomplete and ineffective. A great
many of the old sins were not actually sins. They only managed to

alienate man from his sense of God and self because man allowed them to make him feel guilty and bring him down. On the other hand a great many things not considered sinful brought man down but he didn't recognize them as sins. For instance, nobody thought that pain, suffering, sickness, lack of love, too much play, too much work, too much food, too much or too little of anything, and all discomforts and frustrations were sins, but they separated man from wholeness.

Do you get the point? This is a concept of sin which takes the blame away from man—takes sin out of morality. No one deliberately wants downs. He falls for them out of ignorance. If there is any blame, ignorance is the thing to blame. When we don't blame ourselves, it is easier to groove on our mistakes and find out what they have to say.

Downs are like shadows; they exist on the way to the light. Once we are in the light at the fourth dimension we *are* the light and there are no more shadows. At the fourth dimension there is no sin because we are fully human. On the way we have shadows because they indicate the direction of the light, but they exist to inform us in which direction to head.

All of life is a matter of ebb and flow, of ups and downs. A perfect state of security where there isn't any chance of downs is only a perfect state of stagnation. Nothing grows in stagnation but slime. If we want to be really creative we have to take a chance on downs. Even science tells us that nothing is created without tension, the pull of opposing forces. A ball won't roll on a flat surface.

Downs and hardships are the fertilizer of life. They don't smell nice, in themselves they are not nice, but they do serve a purpose. They make us grow. If we want to grow, we must learn to welcome them. Actually, we should be worried if we never had any downs, or sins, for that would mean either we were fooling ourselves or we were not living creatively and pushing on to the fourth dimension.

Look at your own life. See how almost always your greatest heartbreaks, your greatest trials, your most profound setbacks have resulted in your greatest pushes forward.

We will not progress until we become grateful for our trials and tribulations. Our third-dimensional subhuman self is satisfied when it is at peace, tranquil, and secure with material good, but none of these feelings is real freedom. Spiritual freedom is above bad and good, sin or virtue. Our downs make us want fourth-dimensional spiritual awareness.

Downs bring us another bonus. They make our ups more pure, more sweet, and more valuable.

While we are learning to groove on our downs and not put our downs down, we can add to our growing morality by taking it another step: We shouldn't put *anything* down.

Refusing to put something down in no way implies that everything is allowed to run rampant, that there is no morality. There are hardships we all wish to eliminate.

Those who have learned lessons from the past could help others by their experience, but if they offer their advice in the form of a put-down, they show they haven't fully grokked. Others, particularly the young, won't accept advice from those who have shown by put-downs that they haven't grokked.The young would rather pay the price of hardship in order to grok fully than accept the shortcut of a put-down. Naturally they would rather avoid a rough time if only someone could get the idea across to them in a way they could grok.

Another suggestion might be added to our morality. When it comes to our fellow men: Let everyone off the hook. Whenever we hold another person under judgment, whenever we hold another person responsible, we have him isolated from the world, we have him "hung up." After we have found out what a person is "for," and after we have grokked the whole situation, including our own place in it, we must let the other person off the hook. Most often we are not responsible for the other person anyway, we are not our brother's keeper, so it isn't our business to rush in and throw our weight around unless he has asked us to; so if we turn him over to God and go about our own business, we have let him off the hook.

When it comes to someone with whom we are closely involved,

a member of our family or an employee, for instance, once we have grokked a situation, we will find that the inharmony was caused by someone or something being out of place, not doing what it was "for." When we find what was out of place, we doubtlessly see that ignorance or confusion caused it—and we can blame the situation but release others from guilt. When we can let someone off the hook, he can find himself much more quickly.

Most important of all, we must let ourselves off the hook. When we have stumbled or fouled up somehow, we have to grok the situation in its full dimension, using our minds, our bodies, and our spirits until we experience what it is all about. Then we must find in what way we were not doing what we were there for, and finally release ourselves, let ourselves off the hook. When we realize our true place, we are free from the hypnotism of ignorance, and we are loving ourselves. As long as we have ourselves hung up, we are not part of the living whole, certainly not seeing ourselves as one with life.

An Appetite for Life

We are all stretching to infinity. That's the purpose of being. When the light of day is fully here, when the whole world has been Christed, we will all realize our infinity, but in the meantime we are reaching for it. We are all growing an appetite for life, and as this appetite grows, our ability to partake of more and more life grows. Now that we consciously realize the importance of grooving on the big and the little, on each moment, on each place, on each person and thing, we are taking a very big step toward being fully human. For many, particularly the older generation, this appetite for life is like a muscle which needs daily conscious exercise in order to strengthen it and make it grow. Others, mainly the young, who have been born with enormous appetites for life, need conscious direction and discipline.

Whatever makes us more living, more alive, more fully being, helps fulfill the purpose of why we are here. Anything that makes us less living, less fulfilling our life, is drawing us away from our purpose. So the golden rule of the new morality is: *Anything that makes me more living is an up, and anything that makes me less living is a down.*

Don't be deceived by the oversimple, untheological sound of that principle. It actually cuts right across our old morality. All of the things called bad by the old must now be reexamined to see if they help make one more living, and the old goods have to be checked to see if they don't possibly encourage stagnation.

Far more than just outlining a rule of thumb to live by, this golden rule really defines the difference between the spiritual life and the material sense of life.

People have made the spiritual life far too mysterious. It is really very simple. When I say "spiritual," I am not talking about lighting candles or spouting prayerful incantations to evoke some kind of magical intervention in the affairs of man. I'm talking about a plain old commonplace thing of which we can be aware at any moment we choose. At any moment we can be aware of the spiritual and we can have recourse to spiritual power, because at any moment we can stop and realize what kind of spirit or head we are in, whether we are down, up, happy, sad, angry, negative, or positive. If we learn how to control our spirit, we gain control of our mind and our life and we are spiritual. It's that simple.

When we live in such a way that the spirit in which we do things is more important than the result, we are living spiritually. Results are material, so when results are more important than the way we go about getting them, we are not living spiritually, but when spirit takes precedence over results we are living spiritually.

It could be stated another way which underlines the revolutionary aspect of this new day. Jesus said we are always faced with two facets of life, and he gave us two commandments to follow: the love of God and the love of man, the invisible and the visible. But he said that the first and greater commandment is the love of God—truth, spirit, or the absolute. Until now the lesser, the love of the material,

has been put first and ths greater has been second. Now we have
a completely new day because the young and all of those who are
revolutionaries are reversing the order. We will continue to have
both sides, both the material and the spiritual, but now the greater
will be put in its rightful place and will take precedence over the
lesser. Spirit will come before materiality or results.

The story of Mary and Martha explains it another way. Martha
worked, took thought, planned, and worried about material needs.
When she got fed up with Mary's apparent lack of concern for
household duties she complained to Jesus. He acknowledged the
material need, but he let Martha know, "Mary hath chosen the
better part." In the past our society was based on fulfilling the
material or finite necessities first, but now the spiritual or absolute
will take precedence, though both sides must be taken care of. Now
the Mary in us will be more dominant than the Martha. Nothing
new, just a reversal of importance.

The spiritual life is simple, but it's far from easy. It means that
we can never let our spirit be one of resisting evil, no matter how
justifiable the cause seems. It means that we can never condemn
another person, no matter how evil he appears. It means that we
can never let ourselves get depressed or down, no matter how we
are persecuted. It means that we must never think down thoughts
or perform down actions in order to get what we want. We must
think first of the spirit, then of the results.

When Jesus told us in the Beatitudes, "Blessed are the meek,"
"Blessed are the pure in heart," and "Blessed are the peacemakers,"
he didn't mean that those qualities were good in themselves; he
meant that persons who followed those examples were blessed
because they were in the right spirit and their selves were not being
poisoned by a bad head.

While we are on earth, we won't always be able to live spiritually,
we won't have all highs, we won't reach a point where there are
no "bummers," as the young call things that bring one down. We
shouldn't want all highs and no bummers. When we have fulfilled

our reason for being human and fully realized our oneness with infinity, we will be completely grown and will live *as* the high. Until then, we should be challenged by the hunt for a life with fewer and fewer downs and more and more highs.

When we have experienced the fullness of life—not just bits and pieces of life but life in its fullness, its richness, seen in every experience—we will truly express God. We will be loving life, and that means we will be loving God. We can say, "I know how to love God," because when we grok life we are living, and living is loving God.

CHAPTER TWO

The Identity Dilemma

Life is a juggling act. While we were in the dark, we couldn't see life in its full perspective any more than a juggler can perform in the dark. In order to juggle, we touch only one ball at a time, but we have to keep our objectivity about all the other balls at the same time, touching each one in turn. The ability to keep all the balls in the air is vitally important to those who want to live in the light of day.

When we pay too much attention to one aspect of life, our thinking becomes crystallized, frozen, hung up, up tight, a bummer. In our Morality of Grace, if we let anything become crystallized into an abstract religious theorem or if we become hung up on the material form and lose sight of its spiritual being, we are once more under the mind-controlled world.

At any moment we can stop and ask ourselves: Am I crystallizing this situation, or am I loose and free? If we are one-sided about anything, we can use our new-found guidelines to help us get free once more.

How do we know when we are free? When we don't always have to take thought and are able to live by spirit, we are free. When God is living our life, it only means we are living without having to think up answers, that our thoughts are not self-produced but come bubbling up out of our sense of freedom.

Almost every action we take is motivated out of our search for freedom. Even the most down actions we perform are just mis-guided steps toward freedom. A man robs a bank because of the freedom he thinks the money will give him. A person commits suicide because he thinks his life is a prison and he wants out. People lean on drugs because they want freedom from the physical and mental limitations in which they feel crystallized. The desire all of these people have for freedom is an up, but the way they go about trying to get free may be the down.

Then how do we get free without resorting to downs? There isn't an easy way. We have to practice something which could, if we let it crystallize, become a down. That's why freedom is a paradox: we have to accept something which looks like the opposite of freedom in order to achieve freedom—that is, *discipline*, self-discipline. When discipline is forced, it becomes a down, but without discipline there can be no freedom.

Take, for instance, a ballet dancer, a football player, a scientist, or an astronaut. Such people have attained the freedom to perform the most intricate steps and maneuvers simply because they found discipline to be the key to real freedom. By disciplining themselves with daily exercise in order to build muscles, by learning all the techniques of their professions, they gained control and became free to do what they wanted. But discipline is tricky. If one becomes a slave to discipline, he isn't free to create on his own.

Most of us would like to do without discipline because it has been used as a hammer to hit us over the head, wielded by the old society which wanted us to conform or feel guilty. But we had better learn how to grok self-discipline in our new morality.

When a person accepts a system of control, he is a disciple of that system, like being a disciple of a teacher. When a parent tries to discipline a child into conforming to rules and regulations, he is trying to make the child into a disciple of rules and regulations instead of freedom and self-expression. But when a person believes he will become free by fighting the rules, he becomes a disciple of anarchism and resistance.

If we want to be a disciple of our own whole self, we have to enter a discipline or training which includes three things: responsibility, commitment, and integrity (three words that reek of the old morality and must be redefined for use in our new morality).

First, *responsibility*. Responsibility is a word made up of two words: *response* and *ability*. Responsibility is part of discipline because we do not have freedom unless we are able to respond and unless we do respond.

When older people complain about the young not being "responsible," they are really complaining because the young don't respond the way they *want* them to. Actually, many of the young are much more able to respond with their whole selves than the old are. By responding, the young are responsible. The old often mistakenly think they are being responsible just because they don't break any laws. Actually, many of them are not fulfilling their responsibility to themselves because they have become crystallized and don't know how to respond to life around them. They see the young struggling with a passion for freedom and criticize them, saying that the young are not responsible, whereas the very thing the young are trying to do is to live a life in which they do respond at all levels. Not until the mind-bound people, old or young, discipline themselves into being able to respond fully will they stop being irresponsible.

The discipline of being responsible has another side. Often the young dissipate their ability to respond by overresponding, thereby losing their balance. Sometimes they try to push their capacity to respond through the sound barrier and force it with such loudness, overstimulation, drugs, and the like that they dull their ability to respond on all levels.

A whole person is responsible because he responds both to his own reality and to the reality of others; he responds to both material and spiritual needs. Yes, it takes the whole self to be responsible at all levels, but through discipline, a person can become an astronaut of the spirit.

Second, *commitment.* Commitment and devotion are the same thing. One is the action; the other is the spirit of that action. Everyone who is committed has accepted the discipline of putting his whole self into responding. He has committed or devoted his thoughts as well as his actions and spirit toward achieving the goal. Anyone who believes he can get what he wants without committing himself to it is trying to cheat. He is not taking his whole self into it.

There are things we would like to have or do. We would like to be heroes, we would like to be respected by others, we would like to have a better world. We can have or do all those things and more, but let's not kid ourselves. We can't have or do anything without committing ourselves. But if we commit ourselves to doing nothing, we will end up having nothing and being nothing.

In order to achieve, we must devote ourselves to accomplishing what we want. Theologically, devotion is "the ready will to perform that which belongs to the service of God." Perhaps that is where the word "devout" comes from. Devout means committed. It seems like a contradiction, but we have to be devoutly committed in order to be free.

A ship not committed to a destination flounders in an aimless sea. A person who doesn't consciously commit himself to his personal response-ability to freedom wanders in the dark.

Third, *integrity.* In the past, a person's integrity was based on his ability to refrain from breaking man's laws. If he was law-abiding, he thought he had integrity. Well, he did have mental integrity, but he didn't have spiritual integrity.

Having the desire for freedom and the commitment to it means little unless a person has the integrity to bring his whole self into life. Integrity of the body means keeping one's physical self healthy and ready to participate and using physical effort to achieve one's goal. Integrity of the mind means using the mind without letting it take over, without letting it fear or judge. Mental integrity also includes keeping the mind as a healthy instrument, so it can do its thing when it is called upon. Spiritual integrity means the capacity to keep an up head, to always remember that the spirit of an action is more important than the result.

For instance, there are times when we are committed to a job or to an act of creating, perhaps even to helping or healing another person. If we have lost sight of our commitment and have allowed ourselves to become confused or dulled by dead concepts, drink, down thoughts, or a drug, have become clogged up with a lot of down vibrations, we will be of no use if we are suddenly called upon. Here again is a form of discipline. We must have the integrity to ask ourselves if we are being devout toward our commitment, if we are being responsible, if the freedom we are after isn't more valuable than whatever we are doing that is keeping us from it. We must choose what we want most.

The hardest and most important part of integrity is having the honesty to be ourselves at all times. A person who refuses to put on a face of commitment without being really committed has integrity. A person who refuses to follow laws that he doesn't feel right about in his heart has integrity. A person who is not afraid to stumble and fall if that is where he is at has integrity. A person who is not afraid to respond honestly even though he may be looked down upon by others has integrity. A person who takes on commitments without fearing his inability to fulfill them shows the integrity of self-love.

Making mistakes does not mean a lack of integrity, but when a person tries to act as though he were something other than his state of consciousness, tries to pose as something he is not, he shows by his falseness that he doesn't have integrity. A person who lives up to whatever degree of truth he has found has integrity, while someone else who actually knows much more but doesn't quite try to live up to what he knows has little integrity. He is not true to himself.

That is why the last price, and the most difficult, we pay for freedom is the discipline of knowing our own selves. Unless we know who we are, we can't possibly have the integrity to respond honestly and fully commit ourselves.

Knowing Ourselves

Nine times out of ten, we have lost our freedom and integrity because we have lost our sense of who we are—or we have never known who we really are. When we feel a loss of freedom, we usually try to blame a particular problem or some person who has hung us up, but it may be something simple and ordinary which has tricked us into a false picture of ourself, something as simple and ordinary as a label.

A short time ago a friend invited me to her house for a Saturday afternoon party. As I arrived, and as each of the other thirty guests arrived, the hostess announced a few simple rules for the afternoon. She explained that she had deliberately invited people who did not know each other, people who were all experts in their fields, and that she did not want us to tell our last names to each other or to divulge our professions. We were otherwise free to talk about anything we wanted to. Well, you never saw such a helpless group. There we were, successful people who didn't know how to talk to each other without the identifying labels of doctor, lawyer, merchant, or chief.

The result of the game was that everyone listened to everything everyone else said, no one judged, everyone treated everyone else with respect, everyone was warm and fraternal. The room was full of people, not labels.

If you think you know yourself, ask yourself: Who am I? See how far you get without labels. I did, and I was shocked to see how I had let labels isolate me from the whole world. First I said I was a male, and that cut me off from half of the other human beings because half of the world's population is female. Then I said I was a white male, and I cut myself off from all my black, yellow, and other brothers who are not white; in fact, I cut myself off from all but a fraction of the world's population, for by far the largest percentage of the world is not white male. Then when I added, "I am an American," the noose got even smaller. When I accepted labels for city, religion, age, and so on, I finally isolated myself from the whole world.

Acceptance of labels might seem innocent and harmless except for the fact that once we have accepted them for ourselves, we start living by the laws of those labels, within the confines of those labels, and we are no longer free. The minute we label ourselves anything, be it man or woman, liberal or reactionary, establishment or hippie, old or young, we are cutting ourselves off from pure beingness.

The desire not to be a label has motivated most of the rebellion of the past. Many have rebelled against accepting a professional label which would trap them for life into a single type of job. Many have rebelled against being forced into patterns of life which would routinize them and eliminate spontaneity in life. And many have rebelled against having to live under the label of an ethnic group or class.

Apart from those who have rebelled, many have become aware of wanting to be free of labels by studying books on the importance of one's self-image and how to change it. It is perhaps a good thing to improve our self-image, but ultimately one label is just as bad as another, and we aren't really free until we have gone beyond labels altogether.

Truly knowing oneself is like knowing God—if you have a name for it, it isn't. That is why man has been so often defeated in his quest to know who he is. He can experience himself, but he is constantly changing; so in order to know who he is, he has to keep experiencing his own consciousness over and over. His name means nothing unless he knows what state of consciousness his name represents at the precise moment he is using it.

Basically, the mystics are right when they tell us we are spirit rather than body. If any one aspect of the whole man has to be considered more important than the others, we will have to say that it is man's spirit self. At best, we are that which is functioning the body, making it live, the very life within the body. We are not so much the physical body as that which is happening in and through the body. If we really want to know ourselves fully, we must know that we are what we see with our eyes as well as what we recognize with our minds, and at the same time we must know we are really consciousness which manifests itself as body, mind, and spirit. Our job in life is to be infinite enough to be able to know all aspects of ourselves at once without isolating any single side as though it were the whole of us.

Our goal is to see God as everything including ourselves, but as human beings, we cannot exist in the world without assuming some identity. The problem is that when we have too much personal identity, it turns into egotism and cuts us off from our source. On the other hand, mental institutions are full of people so wrapped up in a sense of the infinite impersonal that they can't identify with self and they have ceased to function at this level. In India some have even experienced a kind of samadi in which they lose their sense of identity to such an extent that they die.

Jesus knew he had no being apart from God's, yet he answered to his name; he said "I" referring to his personal identity, even his body. So what do we do? How do we cope with this dilemma of being both a personal man and an impersonal God?

In this new day, where we don't put anything down, we cope with this dilemma by realizing that being alive is a fluid state. To understand this takes grokking, to insure against crystallizing anything into one-sidedness. Our lives are living, which means that they are constantly on the move, and so is our own sense of identity. At every moment, we are either putting on a covering of personal sense or we are stripping off layers of personal sense. We are never stuck in a perfect state of dead balance between the two.

The best way for me to explain how this operates is to show how it works for me. Every time I get involved in some sizable public activity such as producing a play, publishing a book, or being involved in any public creative venture to which my name is attached,

I go into it with the knowledge that I might have to pay a price. I can't avoid the involvement, feeling I don't want to pay the price, or I wouldn't be living up to my personal integrity by experiencing what life has for me; so I plunge in.

Each time I get more and more caught up in a whirl of personal contacts, public appearances, television, radio, and speaking engagements. Bit by bit, a sense of a personal self grows deeper and deeper. I become more and more aware of myself in relation to other people, in duties to perform, in time schedules where a "me" has to be at a certain place at a certain hour. By the time my duties are completed, I am well aware of a me who now fits a number of labels. It becomes increasingly difficult to get silent within and feel God. I get overaware of myself as a body and mind and uncomfortably unaware of my spirit self.

Having learned the hard way, when I start a project I know not to make commitments any further along than necessary, so as to have time for a retreat on completion of the project. When my activity is over, the pendulum begins to swing in the other direction. My sense of personal self begins to be scrubbed off of me. Naturally, my identity isn't happy with the scrubbing. I go through hell. It's no fun, but having too much personal sense becomes a down and the down causes the purging. So, after a matter of weeks, sometimes dark weeks during which I have to make myself remember to groove, I once more stand naked, or emptied of identity.

Once more there returns the feeling of being lived by a deeper sense of myself than my human identity and with it all the glorious sense of freedom that comes from releasing the world of judgment and separateness. I no longer feel I am a businessman, author, lecturer, or any of the other labels. I am just me—one with God. My moments in meditation become powerful and clear once more.

Then it starts all over again. When I am recharged and transparent, I am once more ready to share. Everything is so groovy I start getting involved again, even though I know what it means to take on self-awareness. That's as it should be, because as long as I am on earth I want to be fully alive. I am always either putting on personal sense which means I will sooner or later have to pay the price of being purged or I am already in the process of suffering the ego loss that I need in order to once more be free and creative.

This example is an oversimplification. However, it applies not only to human identity but to all forms of our creative and spiritual life. Each of us must assume a personal identity in order to work in the world or create. While we work, the awareness of transcendental beingness decreases in ratio as the personal sense increases. The whole process is not a matter of good and bad; it is a creative tension which keeps us from ambivalence, keeps us from dropping out of the world by not being all we should—both man and God at once.

Man of Earth

In order to have the integrity to know ourselves at any given moment, we have to understand both major views of self—our personal Man of Earth self and our spiritual Man of God self. Unless we understand and love both of these aspects of self in their fullness, it is impossible for us to know where we are at any moment as the pendulum of our consciousness swings from one awareness to the other.

Ordinarily, when we talk about the whole man, we are referring to the Man of Earth in his wholeness, which is rather like referring to the trinity in its three aspects. The trinity makes up one whole, but humanly we see it as three parts. The closest we can come to knowing anything or any activity on the finite level is to see it in terms of a trinity of physical body, human mind, and divine spirit.

There are three kinds of Man of Earth, for that matter. Look at the people you know. You will see that each fits one of these three. One person is more body-conscious than anything else. He primarily responds physically and secondarily mentally or spiritually. Another person primarily responds in terms of his mental self, with the physical or spiritual following in importance. Still another responds with spirit first, body and mind afterward. Everyone has all three aspects, but one aspect is always more dominant than the others.

In order to know fully our Man of Earth selves, we have to know the extremes of each of the three aspects of ourselves, almost as though we were seeing ourselves as three different people. When each extreme is understood separately and in depth, it can be reconciled into a whole. Then we can recognize when any aspect has atrophied or overpowered the other aspects.

Body man not only has a physical form which needs to be understood and kept in good shape, but he only responds physically to the things he encounters. Like responds to like. Abstract or mental theorems don't register with the purely physical man. All his responses are physical and come only from physical identification with other persons or things.

Body man can't identify unless he has another body to identify with. In order to learn, he needs a guru or teacher to learn from or to whom he can relate his actions. That is why primitive people and the class of people who are involved with the more physical aspects of life have to have a personal savior to emphasize.

There is no need to put down those who want a physical teacher or avatar. As each one of us includes a physical man, though that side may not be predominant, we all need, at some time in our lives, a personal savior with whom to identify. Perhaps we are guided mentally or spiritually more than physically and feel we don't have to look up to any human being. If so, we may be ignoring the purely physical side of our natures. We will find ourselves operating more wholly if we begin to include a personal ideal. Those of us who shun becoming disciples of a Jesus, Buddha, or even some modern revelator are cheating ourselves out of wholeness. Self-consciousness in deifying another person is the mind's attempt to keep us under its control. We had better get simple and let ourselves personally love a Jesus or a Buddha to be balanced. We may not often have to identify at that level, but at times it is necessary. Accepting a personal teacher with personal identity may be considered the lower corner of the trinity, but it is in no way inferior or less important than the other aspects. Anyone who believes that a physical response to anything is inferior to the mental and spiritual responses is equally wrong. When we eliminate our awareness of the need to respond physically, we are out of balance and it might be good for us to deliberately find ways. Sometimes a physical pilgrimage brings the physical into line. In a simple way, lighting a candle, or saying a personal prayer, may do it. At any rate, not to expect the physical side of man to respond physically or emotionally is a condemnation of part of one's own self. Far too many intellectuals, and far too many metaphysical students, have been tricked into this rejection of their whole selves.

The next part of our whole selves is the mind. Mind man goes wherever he lets his mind go. Anyone who thinks he can be whole by using his body and spirit without bringing his mind into the trip is doomed to wobble on an unsure course. Perhaps physical man is doing his thing by building his churches, participating in rituals, and offering his tithes, but unless his mental side is making every effort to understand the meaning behind it all, he is tangled up in blind faith, and faith that is not balanced with logic is just that— blind, unseeing.

Now, as body man needs a teacher with whom to identify, mind man needs a teaching. Teachings are mental, and naturally the mind identifies with them. To "know thyself" is the highest form of mental expression; to know the absolute self is to know God. So the more absolute the teaching comprehended by a mind, the better.

If mind man hasn't found a teaching he thinks is right for him, he must keep looking. The fact that he continues to use his mind to investigate keeps him whole.

Mind man doesn't have to focus on a Jesus or a Buddha, a human identity, but he has to recognize that it is possible for man to have that Christ or Buddha consciousness within him. He has to be able to see that there was a Jesus , or a Moses, or a Mohammed who had the Christ consciousness. The Christ consciousness is present whenever man has seen himself as one with God—no matter what name it is called by. It is necessary for the mind to accept that this has happened to others so that it too can eventually experience God.

Mind man must also have the integrity, as I said earlier, to keep the mind trained, educated, and not too drugged or cluttered with useless value judgments so that it is ready and able to be called upon when the mind side is needed.

The third aspect of our whole selves is the spirit man. Within each man is the capacity to make contact with the truth of his being, to feel it and experience it beyond the purely mental and physical. Within each man is a "deep well" of peace, or the possibility of resting in a real and recognizable feeling of universal oneness. It's a kind of joy. Joy isn't physical and it isn't emotional; it's a kind of exaltation. If we are not able to experience this peace and joy, we are not whole, not even whole Men of Earth.

That's why laughter is so important. Heavy, dreary "religious" people who walk around in gloom, never laughing, are ignoring their spirit selves; there is no joy. Instead of saying, "Families who pray together stay together," I would like to say, "Families who laugh together love together." There is nothing more beautiful in the world than a family of old and young who are all laughing together. It shows they are a whole family physically there, mentally free, and spiritually full of joy.

Whereas body man needs a religion with a personality at the forefront, and mind man needs a religion with high ideals, spirit man needs the capacity for love or mysticism. Any teaching, religion, or philosophy has to include the possibility of the actual experience of God to be whole. Any teaching that helps its people attain this inner contact is spiritual. A teaching may be mental and it may be physical, but it isn't spiritual if it ignores the need for man to have the mystical experience himself.

Of the three sides, the spirit is usually the last to develop and is the one most needed today in "wholing" up mankind. The advent of man's capacity for the third side is what marked the end of the dark period. Because spirit is light, in the mental-physical day there couldn't be a sense of universal light. That's what the revolution was about—freeing man from the mind and body domination so that all three could make up a whole. The three parts and their manifestation form a kind of triangle within a triangle: body man needs to see a Jesus as God, mind man needs to see himself as God, and spirit man needs to experience God.

I have used religion as an example, but a whole man responds in all his activities with the full trinity of self. If any job or relationship has broken down, he can examine the situation to see if one of his selves is not functioning properly.

For instance, often a person who considers himself a spiritual student will conscientiously study and pray, but he is confused because he has no supply, no money. He will have an abundance

of spiritual feelings but few of the earthly or material things he
wants. This is probably because he isn't responding wholly himself.
Our getting comes from our giving. If we want material things, we
have to give of our material selves. We may not receive back from
the same place where we gave, but we will receive if we give. Even
if we have only "a few drops of oil," as the Bible story goes, we must
"begin to pour." We can begin to pour by something as small as
giving a stick of bubble gum to a child or offering a flower to some
down person who needs it.

We should also contribute at all levels of self to any teacher,
teaching, or activity from which we want to receive. We must
contribute from our possessions, our mind, and our spirit. We are
simply not going to receive from anything we don't give to.

The same applies to our jobs. A lot of people complain that their
work is a drudgery. They are probably offering the job their minds
and bodies but not their spirit and love. No matter how mundane
a job seems, if we offer it our whole selves, if we honor and love
it by taking our fullness into it, the job will honor us back with joy.

Actually, we respond wholly for a very selfish reason. There isn't
any God up in heaven keeping score. The simple truth of life is: if
we want to receive, we create our own receiving by giving, and in
direct mathematical ratio, the more we give, the more we get. We
can receive from a teacher, job, or loved one for a while without
giving from every level, but before long, we shouldn't be surprised
if something takes that person or activity out of our lives or if the
relationship seems to dry up. Wholeness wasn't there. We would
be wrong to think it has happened by mistake or accident; consciousness was at the root.

The Man of God

No one has ever seen the Man of God. He isn't in this world of
recognizable being. No one has ever seen you. No one has ever seen
me. I have seen bodies, I have recognized personalities, but I have
never seen the truth of those people. If you think you have seen me

you are mistaken. I am even mistaken if *I* think that I have seen me. I may have looked in the mirror or seen a form in a photograph, but that wasn't me. Sure, I have had bodies, maybe many of them, but you or I have never seen me by seeing my bodies.

To begin with, I had a tiny eight-pound body when I was born to this name with which people try to identify me. But that body was entirely different from the one they identified me with a few years later, and there certainly is little resemblance to the one I am associated with now.

As for that, reincarnation, the belief that one has many lives, is probably the best known way of explaining that I have been here since the beginning of time and will be here until all eternity. If you guessed at some of my past lives or if you thought I was only this present one, you would be wrong. I can't be known with any faculty you possess. You can experience me, fourth-dimensionally, but you can't know me by any method which differentiates.

Neither am I limited to any nation or place, not even to any planet or universe. I am limited only by the limits of the kingdom of God. I am not limited to being a man. I am not limited to being a woman.

I am perfect, and so are you; I have always been perfect. I have never made a mistake. I have never lacked love. I have never been anything but immortal, God-created, God-maintained, and God-fulfilled, and neither have you . . .

Certainly this kind of talk offends the mind. The mind just can't grasp it. You could well ask, "How can a grown-up man say that he has never made a mistake and never even been seen?" And to anything which speaks as a you or a me, those statements can't be understood. But, as I said before, a human identity with its body, mind and spirit exists at the third dimension, and at the fourth we are our completely naked, self-purged, identityless selves. This fourth-dimensional self lives in silence. It stands face to face with itself only when all words have stopped, all multiplicity is gone, in a state of unconditioned being where all is God. This self is the one which never makes mistakes and is never seen. Surprisingly enough, this state can be experienced.

Perhaps another statement of Jesus' will illustrate. He said, "I am the vine, you are the branches, and my father is the husbandman." And, "If you abide in me, you will bear fruit richly, but if you are cut off, you will wither and die." Well, just point out the window at a vine. What is your finger actually pointing at? It isn't pointing at the vine; it is pointing at a part of the vine. Nonetheless you say, "There is a vine." You can't point at all of the vine at one time, can you? Though your finger is pointing at one of the vine's branches, it is pointing at the vine.

But within that branch is all the life of the vine, all the qualities of the vine, so that the branch is fully one with the vine. It derives all its good from the vine which it really is at the same time that it is a single branch. From one side, we could say that we see the vine when we see the branch in much the same way we say we see a person when we see a body, but both would not quite be true unless we included all the branches of the vine and all the leaves, roots, etc.

In life, that is impossible because infinity is too large to identify, yet you are actually one with that total infinity, so you would have to say you saw infinity before you could say you saw me or anyone else.

Here is how that works: Perhaps there was one seed to begin with. It grew into a vine, and that vine bore thousands and thousands of grapes full of seeds. Many of these seeds fell onto the ground or were carried by birds to other lands. Each time the seeds began to grow, they became vines themselves and in turn produced more seeds and on and on and on. Yet the only life was really a continuation of the spark of life that was in the first seed, not separate lives but the expansion of that one life. So even when you point at or try to identify a whole vine, you are cutting it off from its true self, which is really all the other vines as well.

When we feel we have a life apart from that Christ spirit, we have cut ourselves off from the vine, and when the vine doesn't recognize the husbandmanship of all of life, it becomes cut off.

In another way, though each individual is much more than its individual manifestation, it is still complete within itself. Each grape on a vine is complete in its form and needs nothing from any other grape. Yet each grape finds its completeness from the invisible source to which every grape is connected. Because it is connected to the source, each grape is every other grape, though it is complete in itself.

To humans, or to all beings for that matter, the source of each person is the light, which is God. Each person has a light body which gives rise to the visible body, but the light body itself is invisible. It is the truth of the person, the other end of the wholeness.

When we hear that the search for the self must be conducted within, no amount of mental or physical surgery can help us find it in our body. The part of us for which we must look within is the *I* at the very center of our being. And when we find it, we realize that our spiritual integrity is our ability to turn to that *I* within for all our guidance, our inspiration, our fulfillment. We must realize that this *I* within us needs no man, for this *I* is not dependent on "man whose breath is in his nostrils."

This *I* doesn't have to announce itself. This *I* is an invisible presence that is always with us. At any moment, this *I* is there for us to turn to, inwardly and silently.

Stop . . . right here. Now, forget everything I have just said. Feel what I was trying to say. Feel a presence which is within you. That is the *I* that was being talked about.

To get a feel of that *I* is to enter the fourth dimension. Third-dimensional man is indeed body, mind, and spirit, and we must know and relate to all of those aspects because we do operate in the third dimension much of the time; but actually we are always both dimensions at once. Our ability to comprehend from the fourth dimension is growing greater and greater and will continue to grow until the glorious day when we live fully fourth-dimensional lives.

This fourth-dimensional *I* is not earthbound. It has no limitations. It is the unconditioned self. It is the real spirit self, the universal self.

To think of unconditioned self is one thing, but to experience it is another. That is what makes it fourth-dimensional, because the fourth dimension can only be *experienced*. When we surrender our limited view of ourselves, when we let go of believing we are seeable and knowable, we are loving ourselves fully. When we stop trying to believe we know others, when we see their third-dimensional expressions, we are loving them, we are healing them, and we are praying for them.

The spiritual life is the recognition of the unseeable spirit *I* within. This spiritual life recognizes that the *I* of you and the *I* of me are the same, and if I am and you are, God is. Therefore the recognition of I AMness is the way of love, the life of love, the substance of love. And the secret of mysticism. Now I know what self-respect is. When I have identified with the life source within, I have true respect for myself. When I see with my *I* and not my *eyes*, I know who I AM.

CHAPTER THREE

The Necessity of Others

The first time I heard Oriental music it all sounded alike to me. I was so used to the limitations of the eight-note scale that the freedom and variety of limitless sound turned into one big blur. But when I began to hear and understand the subtle rather four-dimensional quality of Hindu music I got more and more fascinated by its exquisite variety.

The same confusion came over me when I first glimpsed the limitless vistas of understanding that opened up when I was able to understand my third-dimensional self and my fourth-dimensional self. I began to see and understand things I never knew were there before. My ability to enjoy life and to love others became potentially infinite.

At the fourth dimension we are inseparable from all others, so it isn't a matter of loving or not loving—all just IS. But in order to reach that delightful state, we have to start by understanding how to love others at the third dimension.

In order to love others, it is absolutely imperative that we start by loving ourselves. That is why I have so often said that our first responsibility is to our own selves, that every action is rightly a selfish one.

Selfishness is no longer such a down idea when we realize who we actually are, that we are one with all others, just as a branch is one with the vine. But, for the same reason, what we do with

ourselves involves our duty to all mankind. We must think of ourselves first because when we let ourselves get down, in a small way
we are dragging the whole of mankind down with us, and when
we lift ourselves up, we are lifting all of mankind. Jesus said, "I, if
I be lifted up, will draw all mankind unto me," because he realized
he was connected with all mankind in the one body of humanity.
He could just as well have said: I, if I fall down, will drag all
mankind down with me.

Here is where double-thinking comes in. On the one hand, I
must think primarily of myself, for I will be no good to anyone or
anything if I am not healthy and alive at all levels of my being. But
on the other hand, I must think of all humanity, for if I want to be
lifted up, and we all do, then all of mankind has to be lifted, so that
I, by being one with it, will rise with it. I can't just say, "To hell
with the world. I will lift myself no matter what happens to everyone else." Perhaps my consciousness, my head, is high most of the
time, but I am tied to humanity and I personally won't get much
higher until all of mankind goes higher. If I want to stay high, the
whole family of man has to stay high, or I can't rise.

Before long it will seem incomprehensible that in the past we had
to teach people to treat others with love and respect. When the light
has fully come into man's consciousness, we will realize that our
conduct toward others has nothing to do with the old morality of
right and wrong, of having to make oneself be a good instead of a
bad person. We will realize without a shadow of a doubt that we are
joined to all others in one self, much in the same way as we are
joined to our own hands and feet. Everyone knows that an infected
finger affects the whole body. Only our third-dimensional sense of
self, which accepts the illusion of time and space, tricks us into
believing we are not joined with all others.

Anyone who has caught a fourth-dimensional sense of self for one
split moment knows that to commit violence on another person is
like whacking one's own fingers with a hammer or sticking pins
into oneself—real mental, physical, and spiritual insanity. Being

considerate of others isn't good; it's just plain smart and necessary. Absolutely everything we do to any other human being, we are doing to ourselves.

That's why forgiveness and gratitude are so vitally important in the Morality of Grace. Forgiving another person has nothing whatsoever to do with being good or noble. It is a purely selfish act, and a purely necessary one. Whenever we hold any animosity toward another person, we are not loving our own selves. In direct ratio that we feel hate or disgust toward another, we are taking within ourselves a kind of spirit poison because we are bringing our own selves down. When Jesus said, "If you have ought against your brother, go and forgive him before you come to the altar," he couldn't have spoken more simply. We go to the altar to love ourselves; that is a pure impossibility so long as we hate ourselves through hating another.

Gratitude works the same way as forgiveness. Whenever we are grateful to another person, we imply that something or someone besides our own finite selves can bring good into our lives. Our gratitude kills our separateness because it recognizes that we are not alone and cut off, not complete within our finite concept of self. Gratitude actually shows that we know who we are. When we show gratitude to others we are showing it to life or to God expressed *as* the other person. Gratitude is the recognition of the divinity within others and within our own self.

As silly as it sounds, there really aren't any people in the world. There are states and stages of consciousness expressing itself in many different forms, but there is only one self. When we are really aware of that, we see ourselves in all people and would no more think of trying to lie, cheat, fool, or trick another person than we would deliberately try to fool ourselves.

When we realize this oneness, we will automatically know that in life we must contribute to the oneness as well as take from it. Like a community bank account, if too many take and not enough give, the community of mankind goes bankrupt. In fact, that is what was happening, that is what our revolution was all about. We knew we had to jar the mind out of leading us into spiritual bankruptcy.

The Mystical Marriage

In order to contribute my part to the universal bank account I have to understand my relations with other people. I have to know how my Man of God self relates to others and how my Man of Earth self relates. The Man of God is the real truth of myself and a state I will grow into, but by far the greatest time is taken up with my Man of Earth self and its problems. However, without some sense of the absolute I can't design a morality to help my earth self in relation to others.

The whole purpose of the monastic life advocated by the mystics has been to lead man into a state in which he experiences a total absorption in God, his mystical self. In order to achieve this state, it has been believed that a person should cut himself off from all human contact, that a potential mystic should eliminate all human emotion. It has been taught that while a person was in the world of family and business, it was impossible to become unattached; therefore, one should retreat from society and forcibly, if necessary, eliminate any emotional attachment to other people.

When one is locked up in his monastery, the theory implies, the personal sense of self becomes so lonely, so desperate, that it finally lets go and finds its allness in a God sense or God awareness. Then, after having found that, the monk sees God in everything and everyone and never feels lonely again. The supreme relationship of the human world, marriage, is supplanted with the mystical marriage, a total absorption in God. The monk then has a love for all mankind engendered by his love for God.

In theory, that is correct, and perhaps while the world was still in the dark age, man had to go to that extreme to force freedom upon himself, but he did so at a dangerous price. While man was overcoming his attachment to people and things, it became easy to drop out, to condemn the world of humans and to denigrate the value of his own individual personal self, or even to kid himself into thinking he no longer had a personal self.

If the monk succeeded in eliminating all emotion within himself, he was turning himself into a kind of separate elemental being, a brainwashed automaton. Emotion is the carrier for creativity. No creation is performed without it. It is true that misdirected emotion is a dissipation of the spirit, and one of our most important purposes is to direct our emotional power into creative and healing expressions, but eliminating emotion altogether or even shriveling it out of its relationship to other humans reduces us to soul sickness, not wholeness. Emotion directed into an emotional love of a true sense of God has to be felt for all people as well, because that is what God is.

In more modern times, fewer persons have physically tried to force themselves into overcoming human emotions, but many have tried to do it mentally. Many students of certain healing religions have so hypnotized themselves into "un-seeing" human conditions that they have lost all compassion. They have tricked themselves into believing they can live at the level of their third-dimensional awareness while having the nonattachment of the fourth dimension. Instead of realizing that it is possible to go into meditation and experience—the mystical marriage—and then come out and respond in one's humanity, they have accepted the hypocrisy of a double standard.

It's easy to see how they were led into this duality. The established church put so much emphasis on the human and personal side of Jesus that it often ignored the indwelling Christ in each individual man; so the metaphysical church grew in order to remind man of his indwelling Godhead. Then the pendulum swung too far and some metaphysicians threw away the Jesus, the human man, for the Christ.

I personally found this out the hard way. In my panic to storm the gates I forced on myself a kind of monastic life for a number of years. Though I wasn't off on a mountaintop, the results were much the same. At any rate, I ended up facing the age-old dilemma of loneliness. I didn't realize that I had cut myself off from mankind by my lack of empathy for human problems, a coldness brought on by my attempt to rise above emotion.

At the depth of this problem a spiritually illumined friend wrote me, "In your aloneness is your allness." If there was anything I did not want to hear, that was it. But I couldn't get it out of my mind until finally I realized what the mystical marriage was. I realized that once I had an absolute experience of the oneness of God, I would be whole as never before, and then I would be able to feel for all mankind.

Aloneness is different from loneliness. Aloneness is pure oneness. We experience mystical marriage when our aloneness reaches the point where we stop seeing ourselves as separate beings cut off from life and realize our oneness with all.

Each of us, in order to be a whole man and know our Man of God, must at some time in our life experience that total absorption in this divine self. We can do it by a mixture of personal discipline, by a retreat where we go off alone for a period, by an experience we have in meditation, or by living through, and grooving on, some low period life has presented to us. Under grace, there is no one way in which the experience of mystical marriage is brought about, there is no law covering it. It will come because we have recognized it; it will come because each of us has dedicated ourself to being a whole man without eliminating any aspect of ourself. The mystical marriage can take place in a moment, a moment, no matter how short, of the experience of a total absorption in oneness—and each of us is born with the capacity for achieving this mystical marriage.

Perhaps there will be a time when we must deliberately, and even coldly, put the problems of others out of our minds and refuse to acknowledge them for a while. Perhaps we must quote the rather cruel statement Jesus made when he was informed his own mother and brother were outside. He said, somewhat brutally, "Who is my mother and who is my brother? Those who love the Lord." In other words, "Just because they are my human mother and brother doesn't mean a thing. I am not interested in human attachments. My real family are those who have seen the mystical oneness." As for that, Jesus was often rather cold to human problems. On the other hand, he healed and fed the multitudes. He was a whole man.

It is impossible to understand fully a human marriage unless one has caught a glimpse of the mystical marriage—and vice versa.

This mystical marriage has even been explained by science in its own terms. All matter, we learn, is made up of atoms. The only difference between one form and another is the composition or density of the atoms. A rock is a denser composite of atoms than a marshmallow, but basically they are both made up of atoms. We also learn that all atoms are constantly on the move. They go off into the air or move into other substances. A rock may look the same to the human eye for thousands and thousands of years because each atom is replaced by another atom that looks just the same, but nonetheless, the atoms are constantly coming and going.

Scientists say that there are some 5,000,000,000,000,000,000,000,000,000 atoms in one human body, that if these atoms were the size of peas they would form a ten-foot-thick layer around the whole earth and many other planets as well. As these atoms are constantly leaving the body and becoming part of other bodies, in time each one of us has some atoms in our body that were in the bodies of other beings who have long since left the earth.

Each one of us has within us, even humanly, some of the atoms that were in the body of Jesus Christ. By the same token, we have atoms that were in Buddha, Caesar, or even Genghis Khan. Physically we are married to all other being. If we open ourselves to that marriage, in time, like yeast that leavens all the dough, that spirit of freedom which was in the Christ or Buddha can leaven us into the purity that was theirs. This material and spiritual union is the true meaning behind the communion service. By communion, we are married to all mankind.

The Marriage Mirror

That's all well and good. Perhaps it helps me to know those absolutes, but far more of my time is spent as the Man of Earth. I can experience the God man in a moment, but my days are lived facing the problems of my one-to-one human relationships. The infinite me may need no one and no thing, but the infinite me also doesn't think in terms of "me" and "mine"; it doesn't have downs, get lonely, or lose its way.

As a human being at the third-dimensional level, I am not complete and I need other humans to complete me. I need physical contact, mental contact, and spiritual contact with other humans. As a human being, I need the love of at least one other human to form a bridge to infinity. Unless there is another human loving me, I am not linked with mankind and my soul isn't opened to its own creativity at that level.

God is the love I need, but love needs another person to be expressed through at the third-dimensional level. At this level, God cannot be expressed unless love comes through the consciousness of man in terms of his body, his mind, and his spirit. At this level, there are times when the physical affection of another human is necessary, when the mental guidance of another human is necessary, when the spiritual prayers or lifting of another human is necessary.

Though all personal relationships are a kind of partnership, the supreme example and the high point of a personal relationship is marriage. Just as the old morality has broken down in other areas, it has been taking a beating in its application to the institution of marriage as well. If we have a clear new-day understanding of the purpose or need of marriage, we can set about building a Morality of Grace for it.

First of all, no human being can be perfectly objective about himself any more than a picture can jump out of its frame and turn around and look at itself. Our human identity is in a constant state of flux, so if we could have a mirror in which to look whenever we need it, we could have some perspective on the state of our humanness. No one needs to tell the actor how he looks in his dressing room, but he needs a director to be his mirror as to how he looks on the stage.

A perfect marriage is one in which two act as mirrors for each other. Whenever there is doubt, and it can't be cleared up by obtaining an objective state in meditation, another person is needed.

I have known completely dedicated mystics who have left the silence of their retreats to be active in the world. While in the world, each one needed a wife, a husband, or at least a particularly dedicated friend to turn to at times for objectivity about human activities. Perhaps the mystic lacked help only in obtaining objectivity about simple matters, but he needed someone. Often his mysticism made him less objective about material matters than the average person, and he required a mate who was particularly grounded in an understanding of the material manifestation.

Most often we find that two people end up in a marriage with each supplying what the other lacks, and in this way they are infinite in their togetherness. Each mirrors the other.

Our need for a mirror gives us a clue in choosing a mate. If our mate doesn't have the same potential range in his or her scale that we do in ours, it is impossible for that person to reflect back a true total of our image. If the person is a cracked glass or a clouded mirror, he or she can do no more than reflect an image of us that is affected by the cracks or cloudiness, and we are not seeing ourselves, our human selves, in a true perspective.

When we have a mate, however, who has the same range of creative, spiritual, or mental interests, one who looks out on life with more or less the same spiritual values that we do, then we can expect that mate to give us back a reliable sense of ourselves. A mate who is riddled by fear, up tight about security, full of judgment, cannot keep from coloring what he or she reflects back.

I am not saying that the person to whom one is drawn is not the right person because, at some particular moment, he or she does not have the qualities necessary to be a mirror. I am only saying that the relationship has not yet reached the marriage stage. It might be well for the two to make conscious efforts to reach a fuller understanding, to give themselves time to grow before getting married. It may only mean that the right time for the marriage just hasn't come yet, but the chances are that two people rushing into a marriage without an awareness of the necessity of their being mirrors for each other might find themselves headed for more down experiences than they wish.

On the other hand, when two people are suited to mirror each other, a wonderful miracle can take place. You know what happens when two mirrors are held up in front of each other. You have infinity.

In another way, this capacity to "see" a person is the capacity for love. The quality which marks a relationship as a "love affair" is the ability of the two to view each other with love. Each has the capacity not only to see the true perfect spiritual center of the other person but to judge the human aspect accordingly. Because a person is what the world calls blindly in love, he is not necessarily unaware of the human flaws. It simply means that he is aware of the whole person and may be just the right one to enter into a marriage because he could reflect back a whole image of the one he loves.

A word of warning can go along with the capacity to see wholly or reflect wholly. The more God we see in someone, the more possible it is to find faults because the areas in which one is separated from perfection become more obvious. When we see the potential of another, it is easy to expect too much of that person. That is why, as mirrors, we must take great care not to judge, but only to reflect back the picture.

We all need someone to whom we can turn, someone who will have the strength to show us where we are at but who is anchored enough in the spirit not to fall into the old traps of morality, judgment and condemnation. When two people reflect back in the same spirit, they have a spiritual marriage.

The Marriage Responsibility

A successful marriage requires a responsibility, a commitment, that can't be honestly made unless a person loves himself enough not to condemn himself when he is in a down. As long as a person is ashamed to admit being exhausted or out of contact, he can't possibly be honest to the partnership of marriage.

A marriage is a total involvement. Each person brings his whole self into the coupling. Whatever belongs to one belongs to the other. As such, there are not two, only one. Since a marriage under grace is not based on negatives, each partner assumes at all times that his mate is a kind of reserve tank that can be called upon for help whenever he feels a shortage of body, mind, or spirit. A person alone has to be sure he doesn't spend too much of his energy or substance, because he has no reserve apart from himself to call upon, but a partnered person can go right out to the limits of his talents and capacities, because he knows his mate will offer him sustenance when he is exhausted.

The condition is rather like two astronauts in a capsule searching outer space. When one of the astronauts wants to make a space walk, he leaves the capsule with an oxygen tank on his back. If he has ten minutes of oxygen in his tank, he knows he can wander around to the end of his connecting line as long as he leaves himself just enough oxygen to get back to the capsule. There is always a reserve of oxygen back at home base, and his fellow astronaut is there to help him receive it if necessary. Without the assurance of oxygen back in the capsule, he could never go to his full limits because he would always have to save enough reserve, just in case, in order to have time to manufacture more when he got back.

Well, marriage is like that. As humans we attain greater capability or capacity by coupling than by being alone, but we also have a responsibility. And that is to keep our companion informed when we are running in short supply. We go under the assumption that there are reserves ready to recharge us with physical, mental, or spiritual help at all times, so we don't have to remind our partner constantly that we are O.K., any more than we need to remind our loved ones every minute that they are loved . . . they know it. But we do have to let our partner know when we are down in any area.

We have to let him know we are down not only so he can offer us help, but also, and most important, so he won't spend all of his substance without realizing we have no reserve, allowing the whole partnership to go dry. That is why the relationship has to be so honest that each partner will tell the other when he is shaky.

Unless, therefore, we have seen the necessity of downs, have seen that bad periods have their creative necessity, we cannot take our whole selves into a relationship. Unless we have seen that dark periods are part of the whole and we feel no guilt in having them, we cannot refrain from trying to hide our downs from others. If we believe downs are bad, we have to admit failure when we have a down, and no one wants to admit failure. It levies too much of a tax on love. As long as we fear that our partner won't love us if we lack in body, mind, or spirit, we are back in old-fashioned darkness. If we don't inform our partner of our shortages, we might betray the partnership. We must remember that our downs allow our partner to give to us, to love us.

A friend of mine, a teacher and lecturer, carried a rather rough schedule of appointments and interviews. He was able to do this because his wife was a good manager, thereby granting him freedom from household matters to channel his energies to the limits of his talent as a spiritual guide for others.

One day he had a particularly heavy schedule, with a public lecture to be given that night as well. So he left time for himself to take a nap and have a meditation before dinner and the lecture. As it turned out, just as he was finishing his list of appointments, appointments requiring him to share of himself in every way, an unannounced visitor arrived who needed his help. He could not refuse. Out went the rest period, and he drew on his own reserves right up until dinnertime.

When he went to the kitchen, there was no dinner on the stove. He found his wife in the bedroom, resting. She informed him that she hadn't felt well all day but she hadn't wanted him to know because she was so angry at herself for having been weak.

Now this is not a dramatic or serious experience. My friend had enough inner guidance and reserve to pull himself up, make his own dinner, and unstintingly give of himself to those who came to the lecture. But take a look. His wife certainly never intended to harm him or the partnership. Her guilty feeling over being tired or sick nevertheless could have made it impossible for her husband to do his best at his lecture. Had he known she was unable to help him, he could have either canceled unnecessary appointments or cut others short. Then he would have had time for the rest and meditation which he might have needed to open himself in order to be a clear channel for the spirit to work through. As it turned out, this down experience taught them how to make their marriage an even more total experience of oneness.

In a marriage of grace, there is never John's career or Mary's painting, John's intelligence or Mary's sensitivity. Both partners together make up infinity. They are joined. As all of their body, mind, and spirit make up infinity, they work out guidelines with as little "me" or "mine" as possible but with a lot of "our." And when they understand their "our," they form a bridge to all mankind and stretch the family of oneness a bit further.

I can think of no more eloquent or perfect expression of this spirit of total commitment than the one expressed in a hippie wedding ceremony at which I was present. The two who were being joined together were asked to repeat a vow. First the man said, "I promise to remember that in no matter what temporary condition I find my wife I will remember she is a sacred and eternal being." After the girl repeated the vow to him he went on to say, "I promise to commit myself with love and candor to the freedom and fulfillment of her body, mind, and soul forever." I can't imagine a more spiritual commitment.

CHAPTER FOUR

Contact Morality

"Contact" is one of the most important and exciting words in my vocabulary. I am so aware of the necessity of staying in contact with my own inner source (God) and the necessity of staying in contact with other people that the first thing I always do when things start going wrong is to check to see where and how I may have broken contact. It's an exciting word because now that I know I am connected in one way or another with every person in the world, I find it groovy to understand the contact I have with others and to find my responsibility to that contact. Because I have a responsibility (remember, response-ability) to every person in the family of man, I must find out how to respond to each one. Some of my contacts are more personal and involved than others; so there are different things I must do to keep from breaking contact. To understand contact I need a Morality of Grace; I have to understand what keeping contact means.

To explain what keeping in contact means, let us return to our analogy of the vine for a minute. A leaf, an individual, is connected to a stem. Perhaps, as in a marriage, two leaves grow on a single stem, and the stem is in turn attached to a twig where there are several marriages forming a kind of family. Then the twig is attached to a branch making up a whole city of families. The branch is connected to a limb of the vine. This branch with all its cities and all their families forms a kind of nation, and the limb and others tie into the trunk of the tree, joining the whole of mankind. As individuals, we are like leaves joined to the vine of all humanity.

Whatever affects the vine affects each individual leaf, and to some extent, whatever affects each leaf affects the vine. When a leaf gets disconnected from the vine, it naturally withers and dies. When a leaf gets dis-eased, it could spread its dis-ease through the whole vine, so it most likely is rejected by the vine before much damage is done to the whole.

The most fragile connection point is where the individual is joined to the vine. That's why the number one responsibility for each individual is to maintain his own health and keep his own contact. After that, there is a whole chain of responsibilities to maintain contact with our mate, children, family, city, nation, and finally the whole of mankind.

It is easy to find out what keeping contact in a relationship means. All we have to do is ask ourselves what we want "from" the particular relationship. In order to keep the connection alive, we have to give to a relationship what we want from it.

Say, for instance, that you have a "once-a-month friendship" with someone. You want that person to cross your path once every month or so, catch up with interest in what you have been doing, and maybe offer you a laugh or two, then go his own way. If you don't check in with that friend yourself every month, if you are not interested in his doings, and if you don't remember an amusing experience to pass on to him, you are not doing your part and are breaking contact.

The key lies in the word "contact." Our integrity of human relationships depends on our ability to keep from being tricked into disconnecting from those to whom we want to be connected. Of course, some relationships imply a much deeper contact than others, but there is a guideline we can use when we are contemplating an action and want to see what that action entails. We ask: Can I commit myself to this activity and stay healthy? Will the commitment cause me to break contact with anyone I want to stay connected to? If the answer is yes, then we ask: Can I do this without breaking contact with my marriage? Once more, if the answer is yes, we ask the same question on down the line about family, business, partnership, society, the whole of mankind. If some action we are planning might possibly put a strain on any commitment down the line, we can ask ourselves if the value of the action is creatively worth it. If we don't think the plan is worth the disconnecting we can drop it.

In our Morality of Grace, there are some suggestions we can follow to help us keep in contact. We should never go into any relationship without realizing to what degree we are being hooked up with others. Naturally, the supreme involvement is the total relationship of marriage. Such absolute commitment requires that contact be kept intact at all times. It's not a matter of clock time, because two people who are supersensitive to each other can develop an inner ear or spirit link with their mate so that they know if they are in contact even though they might not see each other for days.

Another commitment which many enter without enough serious consideration is the relationship of business partnership. Though a business associate is not a part of one's immediate family, he directly affects the well-being of the family. Through a business, a man expects to feed himself and his family, if he has one. The physical, mental, and spiritual conditions of the partnership will doubtless affect the outcome. Once a commitment is made to a partnership, both partners are humanly and psychically hooked up. They take on each other's vibrations and carry a mutual load.

Before entering a partnership, we can ask ourselves: Am I and my future partner ready and able to commit ourselves in the same manner and to the same degree? Does my partner have the capacity to operate with the kind of spirit with which I must operate to be healthy? Does my partner understand his responsibility to this commitment as I do? Is he taking his whole self into it as I am intending to do? And most of all: Am I ready to commit my own health and that of my family to this partner? If the answers lack a rather strong degree of affirmation, it would be wise to look further before hooking up with him.

Any business we hook up with, whether a partnership or a corporation, affects our contact with life in all kinds of ways. Involvement in a business whose product is designed for destroying human life or for messing up people's heads affects our own head. We haven't realized what contact means if we become involved with down products. The outside and the inside are one. A person is one with the thing he produces.

Though family and business commitments are the most serious ones we enter, every relationship right on down the line to the most casual implies a degree of hook-up. Some hook-ups affect our security to a large degree, others to a small degree. If we want a lot out of a relationship we have to be prepared to give a lot to it. We must always enter a hook-up with the same degree of importance we place on what we want from the relationship. When we want little from a contact we are not committed to stay in close contact, but if we want much from a contact we must be prepared to do our part to keep the contact strong.

If another person wants to enter a degree of contact with us or if we see him unconsciously assuming a commitment which we are not able to enter or do not want to be involved with, it is up to us to level with him and let him know we are not going to become involved with any commitment we are not prepared to fulfill.

Threats to Contact

We can sit down right now and go over our commitments to see if unintentional disconnects or wrongly understood contacts have put a strain on our present relationships. After we have asked ourselves what we expect from a friendship or relationship, we can see how we may have betrayed that relationship by breaking contact.

In friendship, simple friendship from which we want no more

than mutual appreciation, we betray the friendship when we remove ourselves by judging the other person; we break contact when we try to maneuver the other person as though he is separate from our own selves; we disconnect when we try to use the friend for our personal advantage or to fulfill our own personal desire without thinking of his likes.

A university student I know had built up a really beautiful relationship with his grandmother. There was an amazing lack of generation gap. Each respected the other, and each was wide open to face life without judging in terms of the old morality; but something happened that gave the relationship a temporary setback.

One day the student called up his grandmother, who lived a few miles from the university, and asked if he could come to dinner. The grandmother responded honestly and said she was a little low that evening and thought it probably wasn't the best time, but the grandson reminded her it was her birthday; so she acquiesced and agreed to cook dinner for him and a couple of his friends.

Now, from the conversation, the rules of the game were established. He knew that his grandmother needed some support that night, and he had implied his trip was for the purpose of sharing the personal moment of a birthday. As it turned out, he and his friends got to the house and went straight to the game room. One of them had brought along some marihuana that had been given to him. With curiosity, the three students, who were certainly not old hands at smoking pot, tried it out and succeeded in getting stoned.

In the meantime, grandmother was in the kitchen spending her energy cooking for three hungry men. When dinnertime arrived, they came in giggling under the influence of the marihuana and, instead of acknowledging the grandmother's presence, gobbled at the food. The grandmother was sensitive enough to realize that something unusual was taking place. She was honest enough to show her annoyance.

Since the boy's relationship with his grandmother had always been an honest one, and he had confidence that though she might not agree with him in all the things he did, she would not judge him but would offer him her advice and understanding, he explained what he and his friends had done.

Grandmother blew up. You might think that she blew up because her grandson was using a drug, or because he had dared to use it in her home, but that wasn't the case. She sensed that they had broken contact, so she demanded that the boys leave the house; in fact, she put on quite a scene herself.

The grandson returned to his school, knowing that something serious had taken place in his relationship with someone who was very important to him, not because of a family relationship but because of the love and understanding he needed. Since he was one of those young people who are looking for a new kind of guideline based on a new morality, he spent days struggling with the answer to his disastrous evening.

Finally, he came up with the truth. He had broken contact with grandmother because he had used her, used her to cook dinner for him, without giving her something in return. And he had also disconnected himself by smoking marihuana while she was not on the same trip, thus making contact impossible. He realized that her actions were not just old-fashioned fear of drugs but honest reactions to the betrayal of his deliberate disconnect.

The story has a happy ending. The realization of what he had done made him visit his grandmother again, at which time he vowed never to use her without giving in return, never to visit unless he expected to communicate. He also saw how drugs had tricked him into a violation of love, into breaking contact.

I guess we have all experienced the annoyance of being in the presence of a friend who is drinking when we are not. The alcohol affects his vibration or psyche, and he starts communicating at a level where we are not. He breaks contact with us. Our annoyance isn't a judgment of the drinking, or shouldn't be: it is a recognition that he has disconnected from the commitment of friendship for that moment.

In the parent-child relationship, there are many ways we break contact without realizing it. They are not just those of a child's acceptance of security from the parents without the child's fulfilling his side of the bargain. Often parents disconnect from their child by betraying the growth of the child without realizing what they are doing. Children need a chance to grow by stretching. The young come to a time when they need to rebel in order to grow strong, need to test themselves against tough goals. If the parents always agree, always make it easy, always let their children do anything they want, they don't make it necessary for the young to dig deep within themselves and learn. Instead of keeping contact, the parents disconnect from their part of the relationship by not helping the child stretch.

Perhaps old-fashioned fathers were too tough on their sons, but this often made sons strong. They had to become strong enough to stand on their own two feet. When parents make it too easy for their children, it is because they fear and are insecure themselves. This lack of self-love is an actual break of contact with their children. A common mistake is the belief that the young want it *easy.* They don't. They want it *honest.*

There can be a disconnect in the relationship with a teacher or religious instructor. We break contact when we don't level with him, when we withhold our true feelings or thoughts. We disconnect from a teacher when we give him lip service but don't try to practice his teaching. We disconnect from the relationship when we take without giving.

We connect in a relationship when we use our strengths and energies with consideration of others and their needs.

We connect when we fulfill our commitments.

We connect when we are sensitive enough to keep in touch with others, when we remember small pleasures that delight them, when we answer our mail. In short, we connect in a relationship when we communicate or when we create a situation which makes communication possible.

Anything that constitutes a connect is an *up.*

Candoring

When we feel that we are about to break contact with someone and want to avoid it, we can do several things—things which involve our whole selves.

First, we can use our minds for better understanding: we can be candid. To be candid is to be "frank, outspoken, open, sincere, without reservation, disguise or subterfuge, straightforward, honest, and impartial." That's quite a bill. We cannot even begin to approach real candor without applying our whole selves.

However, while our Man of God self is trying to make its inner contact for guidance, our Man of Earth self can sit down with our friend, member of our family, or associate with whom we are in danger of losing contact, in an effort to level with that person and be as candid as possible. If he can do the same, perhaps the unintentional disconnect can be avoided.

That act of attempting total communication with another person is rather like an act of mutual grokking. It means a lot more than just reasoning; it means more than analyzing facts. Mutual grokking requires an honesty about oneself and a willingness to offer oneself with faith. When everything is out in the open and ignorance leaves, love is reestablished.

James Leo Herlihy, the novelist, invented a word that perhaps he will introduce to our vocabulary. He arrived at the realization that it was vitally necessary for him to be candid in his relationships with others and that when his friends were candid with him, they kept in contact. So he took the word "candor," a noun, and turned it into an active verb. He called the act of being candid *candoring.*

Whenever a shadow comes over any of his relationships, he says, "Let's candor each other," meaning: Let's groove on each other, let's open our hearts with love, let's see that any lack of communication is not due to lack of love but rather because some ignorance is trying to insinuate itself on our friendship.

There is one catch to candoring. Like grokking, it can't be performed by people who are still living under law. Candoring is
purely a part of the life of a revolutionary. Anyone who still has to
judge in terms of bad and good, in terms of separateness, can't
candor. You see, we do indeed use the mind as part of candoring;
so if the mind is still trying to be the whole show, if the mind is
full of judgment, it can't candor. By the same token, while we are
using the mind for candoring, we are candoring with our spirits,
and we are offering our bodies to the act.

The spirit of candoring is a positive one or it isn't candoring. We
candor not to prove a point, not to get our way, not to resist an evil,
but rather to keep truth present so love can flow freely. Candoring
is the act of deliberately meeting in person with someone for the
realization of oneness by communicating.

The responsibility for candoring is two-sided. Older people, in
candoring with the young, need to let go of their positions of
authority and see themselves free of age, as ageless as the one they
are trying to candor with. They must keep an inner ear constantly
tuned to the spirit of the meeting and the vibration or feeling of it.
They must make every attempt to leave yesterday out, as well as
their concepts of good and bad.

The young have to try to candor with the old. All too often they
have been slapped down by the old, so they have stopped trying to
candor. They have to realize that it is often harder, not easier, for
the old to candor. The old have more to lose. They are carrying
more mental baggage and have more theories to defend. So the
young have to keep trying, have to educate their parents to what
candoring means, since candoring or grokking is new to this generation.

We have to realize that in being candored, we are apt to hear
some things that make us uncomfortable, and that we must bear the
discomfort, write it off as one of the costs of a real and vital relationship.

When the young just shake their heads and refuse to speak, when they feel unable to candor because they don't have enough words to use or they feel tongue-tied, they are not doing their part as revolutionaries. They must deliberately ask for candoring with their friends and parents and make every effort to offer their whole selves. They must connect.

It seems incredible that we have to be reminded that we need to communicate and keep in contact with each other, but we do, and now that we understand the whole man, we have to remember that communication has many sides. When communication or contact breaks down, it is like a red light signaling us where to put our constructive energies. After all, sometimes even disconnects are necessary for health. You prune a tree at times in order to make it healthier. Don't forget, right now we are in a transitional period. We break contact in many ways we haven't recognized in the past. Each time we bump into a disconnect, we can grok it; then if it involves other people, we can candor with them and reinforce the connection. Eventually the light will shine strong and solid and we will stay in contact.

The Energy of Love

In order to understand disconnects in an absolute sense, we have to understand energy in an absolute way. In the last chapter, I said that in absolute terms no one ever sees you or me. We are that which is happening through the body. We are the flow of energy. Every moment, energy is flowing. In order to know us, someone has to see us as energy rather than as body.

Modern physicists have done a remarkable job of scientifically proving that man isn't body, that we are more accurate when we don't see people in physical terms. Until now physics was constructed on the belief that matter existed, but most advanced modern physicists have discarded the old theories based on matter and have supplanted them with theories based on the knowledge that everything is energy. Their advanced theorems are based on the fact that regardless of what the misguided visual sense beholds, we are only seeing energy formed. No bodies, no things, all energy. Actually, the mystics have said the same thing for thousands of years. Even now Christian Science and other metaphysical teachings are predicated on the idea that everything is spirit—or energy formed. When spiritual contact is broken, its appearance as body gets sick. When the flow of energy is short-circuited, we become disconnected from the true self.

Another way of explaining energy is to equate everything in terms of vibration. Vibration is only the movement of energy. Many young, in a kind of subconscious realization that everything is vibration, often talk about places and people in terms of vibration. They say, "The vibration of that place was down," or, "He sends out groovy vibes." In comprehending life as vibration or energy, the young are showing their capacity to relate to the world in terms of its unity and wholeness. "Vibration" is not just a slang term for expressing old-fashioned judgments. It can be used to point out that contact is intact or has been broken, that someone is experiencing an up or a down.

In the past we often sensed things by vibration but didn't consciously recognize we were doing it. We said, "My first impressions are always right," or, "I should have followed my first impression." At first we sensed the vibration of a person or situation. But often we let our minds think us out of following our feelings. Our minds clouded the truth with their judgments.

Contact morality depends a great deal on our capacity to see ourselves in terms of energy or vibration. If we do, we can find how we have unintentionally misdirected our energies.

Since man is body, mind, and spirit, he has three kinds of energy. There is the plain physical energy of the body, the energy he needs to make his body perform. There is mental energy; the act of thinking uses mental energy. And there is psychic or spiritual energy, needed to keep man in contact with his source of being. A disruption of any of these energies causes us to lose contact.

Most people are very aware of their physical and mental energies. They take great pains to keep from wearing themselves out physically so that they won't feel miserable and become overexhausted. They know better than to work for too long a time without resting or to spend too much time with people who physically exhaust them. Most people realize they have only a certain amount of mental energy. They are aware that a few hours of hard mental work can be more exhausting than many hours of physical labor. They avoid being around people whose minds are uncomfortably overactive. Many businessmen realize they have to give their mind a rest, so they take time off to play golf. Their golf is a necessity for wholeness.

Until now, however, we have not generally understood or recognized our psychic or spiritual energy, so we haven't realized the importance of protecting it. We have let people psychically drain us and we have let ourselves spend too much time in places with a spiritually down vibration, not realizing that we were being used up spiritually. Just because places and people didn't hurt us mentally or physically, we thought we were safe, but actually our spirits were being affected. Of course, if we are strong enough, we can go anywhere without danger because when we feel ourselves getting brought down we can recognize it and leave. At times we might be so full of spiritual energy that we can lift a down person or place into our high vibration.

Meditation, which we discuss later, is the main way to build up spiritual energy. Jesus showed us this by his own example. When he found himself spiritually drained, he knew he could no longer help those who needed his strength. So he went off to the mountaintop to be recharged. Buddha also taught that meditation was the way to recharge.

I could have said that Jesus and Budda meditated to get recharged with love. Spiritual energy and love are the same thing. Of all the energies in the world, love is by far the most powerful. A loss of love can cause the greatest disconnect, but its presence has the capacity to harmonize, to build, to create, and to connect like no other energy. In fact, love is the energy which will one day save the world.

Man has never been able to understand love because he has seen it as an emotion or a thing, and it isn't. *Love is an energy,* an invisible energy. It is the very essence of energy; it is cosmic or spiritual energy expressed visibly. Love is the only energy capable of harmonizing or connecting all of mankind into oneness.

Look at common ordinary friendship, for instance. Friendship unites people. Through friendship, the energy of love is used to bind people together. Through a sense of love energy, man stops being alone and self-centered. He finds himself joined to others and to the family of mankind—purely through the magnetic force of the energy of love.

Because love is the most powerful and valuable energy, the only one which can save us and therefore the whole world, we must take every precaution not to do anything to jeopardize our ability to love. By that I mean if we dissipate our spirit by pointlessly drifting into down associations which cause us to squander our capacity to love, we are not directing love for the purpose of union with others.

In an absolute sense, God is love. In a personal sense, love is the energy of God when it is seen in personal terms. They are the same; one is unknowable because it is infinite, and the other is recognizable because it is expressed in a finite way. We experience God when we experience formless love, but at the third-dimensional level, we can only love God when we love our neighbor. To waste our energy of love by misdirecting it is to waste our contact with God, the ultimate disconnect.

Under law, "wickedness in high places" has to do with the mind and its control over a person. Under grace, "wickedness in high places" has to do with the dissipation of the energy of love. When we place ourselves in a position where we dissipate our psychic energy in such a way that it brings on a disconnect from our responsibilities to ourselves, our families and mankind, we are in the worst of downs.

It takes great energy to candor, including the energy of love, so we must constantly stand watch on our energies. Without falling under the old morality, we can at any time check in with our whole selves to see if we are letting any of the three aspects of our personal energy run low. If so, something is out of balance, and we can feel or listen for ways to repair it. We can consciously do this—in fact, we *must* consciously do it—if we wish to stay in contact with wholeness.

We can consciously look at every person, place, thing, or happening and see it in terms of energy, of the three energies. The list is infinite, and we may take many years defining the new world in terms of energy, in freeing the world from a material concept of life.

CHAPTER FIVE

The Puzzle of Sex and Drugs

Ever since man started trying to put together the jigsaw puzzle of his human existence, sex has been the most complicated piece of the puzzle to fit in. He couldn't ignore sex, but he couldn't make it fit into the puzzle without forcing it into place by rigid laws. He knew that sex had him trapped, but he didn't realize that if he saw the true meaning and purpose of sex it would fall naturally into place. Instead of being his problem it would help him finish the whole puzzle—whatever can trap a person can free him.

Sex has been man's most powerful problem because it deals with man's most powerful energy—love. The energy of love expressed in physical terms is the energy of sex. As I said earlier, love is the energy which will eventually unite the whole world, just as in personal terms it expresses itself in the uniting of two people into oneness. **139057**

Love is a miracle. It's *the* miracle. The bridge between the invisible spirit and the material form is the miracle behind all that man ever calls miracle, and the miracle takes place every time the sex act is performed with spiritual union, love, and commitment. Through the sex act the fourth dimension can be brought into the third dimension. If the sex act were a physical phenomenon alone this could not happen.

The act of our parents by itself didn't give us visible form. It took a spark. Something had to light the third-dimensional fire. Through sex that fourth-dimensional spark comes to the surface. The rest of the time it stays hidden in the invisible. That's the miracle of life.

The spark, the miracle, is given to us not only for procreation but also for *re*-creation or regeneration. Our creative drive is used to generate more being—a baby, a work of art, something that will make the world free—or to regenerate a human being, fill him with life and vitality. Generation and regeneration are two blossoms on the same bush. Both charge people with new life.

The energy of life expressed through sexual love can be directed toward making the world more sensitive to beauty, to joy, and ultimately to the procreation of the spiritual instinct in man. Through the energy of love expressed sexually, men and women can draw others into a more living sense of the spiritual capacities of their natures. In fact, when sex comes from love it can open a person up to his spiritual capacities. Sex can be a valuable part of fulfilling the person spiritually.

By fearing sex, by condemning sex, and by not realizing how spiritually important it is to man, many have been deprived of the generative and regenerative values as well as the spiritual link involved in the physical expression of the energy of love. If mankind is to be whole we must spiritualize sex. We must eliminate the duality of separating sex from the miracle of life. We must understand sex and not be confused by it.

It isn't altogether man's fault that he has been confused about sex in the past. Because he lived by law, he couldn't see that what was adding to wholeness one minute might be a disconnect the next. Marriage had a different sexual purpose in the past. Now the main purpose of marriage has changed. In the past we were a people-needing world; we needed to populate the world, so the prime purpose of sexual relations was for reproduction, to populate the world.

That isn't so any longer. We do not need greater populations. The need now is for the energy of sexual love to be used for making the world more sensitive to beauty, to joy, to the fulfilling and regeneration of our loved ones. Through the energy of love expressed sexually, men and women can draw each other into a more living sense of the spiritual capacities of their nature. When love is present, sex can be a way of lifting and healing.

Today we are ready to communicate at deeper levels of our being than ever before, so sex can be a supreme expression of soul communication. When two people bring their whole selves into sex, a circle is completed and the same miracle which brought them into the world as babies can lift them into spiritual freedom.

That is what sex can do when it is in its right place, doing what it is "for." But if the circle isn't complete, if there isn't wholeness, sex can cause a disconnect. We can't just rush out and bring all the fulfillment to the world of which love sexually expressed is capable. Unless the inherent miracle is vastly respected and nourished it can instead seem to separate man from his source of life, can anchor him more to the third dimension and the material level.

Most of us are familiar with ways our thoughts and feelings on sex can bring us down to a material sense of life. For instance, if someone is sexually frustrated, if his mind has tricked him into thinking he is not complete without having some sexual contact with a particular person, at a particular time or place, if he wants a relationship with someone who has no love for him, he becomes terribly aware of his body. His body becomes a prison, torturing him; he feels cut off from life. When he becomes extremely body-conscious, he certainly can't get free enough from his body awareness to meditate and achieve a fourth-dimensional experience of pure spirit.

But unless we want to revert to the old duality of law, we must realize that perhaps even sexual frustration has its purpose at times. Unless we have fully arrived at a realization of our wholeness, we may become mired down in stagnation without sexual frustration to push us into getting involved, push us into the necessity of finding the truth.

Remember, we are talking about the third dimension now. At

the fourth dimension there is only oneness and no problem. What we need is a Morality of Grace which applies to sex and can instruct us in the basic principles behind the sexual impulse at this human level. Then we can know when sex is fulfilling itself as a means of uniting us with wholeness or when it leads us to breaking contact with ourselves and others.

The key to a morality of sex is the remembrance that sex is basically the energy of love. We have a lot more of this energy of life than we may imagine; so we often spend it without realizing we are doing so. When sex is fulfilled with love, no strain is put on our contact—exactly the opposite, our contact is strengthened—but sex without love can be a spending of the energy of life without receiving in return.

We haven't yet grown to the point where we consciously understand this life energy; so we are often not consciously aware when we have used too much of our self. One of the ways we know if we have depleted our self is if our sense of joy is down, if our creativity is dulled, if we feel tempted to fight the world, if our appetite for the spirit is low. When that is the case, more short-circuited sex can just take us further down, but by the same token real love can restore us. It's not a matter of good and bad; it's a matter of knowing ourselves and the place of love in our life.

Most often when we think we want sex we really want love. When we are attracted to someone physically we think we are turned on sexually, but what we are really starved for is love, the energy of love. Even if we were to have a physical relationship with the person we desire we would still feel frustrated and unfulfilled unless the circle of love was complete.

When two people are forced into the same marriage bed by the old morality of marriage license though they no longer love each other, the two are being forced into spending themselves without receiving the regenerative good that their contact should bring to them. On the other hand, when two people see the God within each other, recognize love in each other, are committed and express the energy of love in a mutual relationship, they are truly married, license or not.

Love is not a matter of time. It doesn't have to take a year or a month or any long time to feel and recognize mutual love, but it is a very tricky matter. We all too often get desire mixed up with love, and we can jump into a down sexual experience mistakenly thinking we have qualified, that we love.

So what guidelines can we use as Man of Earth? To begin with, we can make two tests. First, in pursuing the steps which may lead up to a close and rewarding union with another person, we can ask ourselves if we and they are able to take our whole selves into the relationship. We are body, mind, and spirit. We know we can take our body into a relationship because we feel attracted to the other person. We know we can take our mind into it if the other person is someone with whom we can share thoughts and interests, even spiritually minded thoughts. We know if the vibration or spirit of that person is the kind of spirit we want to have union with, if his spirit is loving and can take flight.

The second necessity is the most important. For sex to be in the right spirit there must be *commitment.* Sexual relations without commitment, without the commitment to give, unite, or make whole, become a separating rather than uniting experience. Commitment has to do with the *self* of the other person. Commitment is made to the oneness of self—not inferior or superior, but one. Finally, commitment has to do with the miracle that is in a relationship.

One doesn't have to be committed in order to derive pleasure from sex, but commitment is necessary if growth is to occur and if true joy is to be experienced.

Understanding Our Sex Selves

In committing ourselves to the fulfillment of another person, we can start by realizing that we are potentially one with infinity. Each of us has a degree of both male and female qualities within us. When we reach infinity there won't be any degrees, we will be all, but on the way we have more of one quality and less of the other. A man usually has many more male tendencies in him than female, and a woman has more female than male.

In the regular course of things, a person is attracted to another person who he feels is strong in the areas in which he is weak and vice versa. Each person is reaching out to wholeness and is drawn to those whose qualities will balance his. Extremes attract extremes, and as balance is reached, a balanced person is attracted to another balanced person.

That sounds awfully clinical, but we can actually see an example of it in the changes that are taking place in our society. Today many of the young, who are realizing a greater degree of the infinity of their being than their predecessors, are beginning to look alike, act alike, and even dress alike. A growing number of unisex clothing stores offer clothing for sale which can be worn by either men or women. In every way they are participating with a high sense of equality.

On the other hand, in the guise of equality a number of people have confused equality with sameness. This confusion has led to much frustration. More simply, when we do not know ourselves fully, we often feel a confusion of roles. Man often doesn't know what it means to be man, and woman doesn't always know what it means to be woman. When man understands which of his actions are predicated on his male instincts and which are predicated on his female ones, he can be clear about his responsibilities and how to fulfill them. When he is called on to express his male qualities, he can do so without confusing the roles. The same is true for women.

The confusion of roles has mainly to do with a confusion of strengths and abilities, but it also manifests itself sexually and causes problems in marital relations, because in accepting the belief that we should be all one way or all the other, we leave no room for the roles to change from time to time in a natural fashion.

We must be aware of what the male and female qualities represent in order to know how to fully be ourselves. Traditionally, the male in a person represents the creative spirit, the invisible source which creates out of the imagination rather than from the visible body. The female side is that which represents the word made flesh, the material or visible which is seen in ways you can see and touch. These two qualities are reaching out toward each other, trying to join, like two pieces of metal being magnetically attracted. They are not duality. They are polarity—two aspects of the same.

If the male side of us doesn't recognize that the female side is the symbol of the earth, the love of the visible world with all its short-comings and problems, we don't comprehend our true love. We spend ourselves wastefully without making the world a better place in which to live. That is why the male in us has to find out all of the secrets of science and the universe. We must love the world, the female.

If the female side in each of us doesn't let go of its worship of material substance and wholly give itself by recognizing the God within, the creative spark, the male consciousness, we spend our energies by placing a false value on material security and don't love the male.

Because society didn't love itself in terms of wholeness, the problem of homosexuality grew. As we all have a degree of both the male and the female within the infinity of our being we all feel a degree of affection or attraction to members of our own sex. This attraction is most often no more physical than a warm handshake or a loving pat on the cheek and not something we recognize as being sexual, but it is a form of physical attraction. When women admire each other's figures or men horse around enjoying some athletic competition, they are expressing this attraction.

In the past if a man felt consciously attracted to his fellow man, or wanted to openly show affection, he was forced into dishonesty. He either had to refuse to admit to himself that he had any affection or attraction, or if he admitted it to himself, he had to think he was a homosexual. Since our society condemned homosexuality as being "queer" or "perverted," he had to think of himself as sick. When man believed that being attracted to another man was sickness, he saw himself as sick, as a sick homosexual, cut off from society. By believing he was sick he broke his contact with wholeness and was sick.

When a man is unable to have a lasting relationship with a woman or when he lets sexual frustration keep him from becoming attached, his alienation may stem from the same cause which leads a lot of people into homosexuality. In an obviously materially changing time, there is a fear of material involvement, fear of being swamped by materiality. Since woman represents material involvement, a man turns away from her or from being attached because he doubts his ability to take on responsibility. He turns to promiscuity or to other men for sex because he feels that this way his manhood isn't threatened.

Because man, in the male sense, dominates materiality, some women become frigid or turn to lesbianism out of fear. They fear being materially destroyed by man in a world in which men are unleashing such powers of destruction. Because of a lack of belief in herself, a woman may be afraid of sexual relations with man in which she might be called on to give birth to wholeness.

Some historians claim that widespread sexual promiscuity and homosexuality brought on the fall of such civilizations as the Roman and Greek. They point out fearfully that the widespread promiscuity and homosexuality today are bringing on the fall of present-day society. Such people are putting the cart before the horse. They don't understand the sexual frustration of many people who, consciously or unconsciously, feel threatened by the changing times and are reticent to be involved in domestic responsibility. Promiscuity and homosexuality are the result of the changing times, not the cause.

We will be confused about the true meaning of sex and its effect on our life as long as we believe that the sex act itself is a cause. The sex act is the result of man's life force expressing itself. No matter if it is a misuse of sex or the proper fulfillment, the actual act is the result of an inner cause. Sex itself never broke up a home or caused a man's ruin. Rather, the disconnect with life or God brought on the sexual frustration, which in turn broke up the home. The energy of love was misdirected. Sex was only the physical expression of that energy.

Never forget, everything that appears at the third-dimensional level is an effect. Even the sex act is an effect; sex itself is an effect. When we believe that it, an effect, has power, when we give it power, we are not free. I guess if there is anything "bad" about sex it is that it had the power to trick us into believing there is a cause other than our own spirit of love.

When we act out of desire which isn't predicated on love, we are grabbing at the fruit of life. We may even be cutting down the tree to get at the fruit. Sex is the fruit of love. It's the reward for having the capacity to love.

Doing a Natural

Ever since man discovered his body he has been confused about sex. Now that man is discovering his soul a new confusion has risen, confusion about drugs. Drugs have been around for a long time without any massive concern on the part of the public, but drugs, all the way from aspirin to LSD, are woven into our way of life, and mankind is having growing pains finding out what drugs are all about.

Nothing takes place by accident. If drugs have become important it is because they represent something significant that is taking place in the inner consciousness of mankind. After all, drugs themselves are effects. They are the result of a need man had within or he wouldn't have manufactured them. Like anything man can identify at the level of phenomena, drugs are a part of the third dimension. We could wear out typewriters compiling lists of bads and goods, of laws to regulate, of theories and opinions about drugs, but that wouldn't help us form a Morality of Grace pertaining to them.

We must not sit in judgment but rather try to understand them.

The psychic drugs are a new phenomenon for society in general because now is the first time that society in general has awakened to the fact that we are not necessarily prisoners of our bodies and minds, that we have a soul which is demanding the light.

Mankind, and particularly youth, is not going to sit back and wait for freedom. Unless the youth are presented with a better way of breaking the mind's hold on them, unless they are convinced that there is another way of self-expansion which won't just bind them back into patterns of judgment and self-denial, they will explore what drugs can do, because obviously drugs can drastically liberate one's head from the brainwashing it has been conditioned by—fortunately or unfortunately, both the good and the bad brainwashing.

Remember the old vaudeville song, "How are you going to keep 'em down on the farm after they've seen Parie?" Well, it is rather like that. Many today have caught a glimpse of the spirit, a glimpse of the high that man will one day live in. How can anyone expect them to now sit still and be satisfied with a structure of society which asks—no, demands—that they live in a low simply because society doesn't know what freedom and highs are?

Whereas Daddy drinks whiskey to give him the courage to compete, to go on the make, to cope with the values of a competitive society, Junior takes drugs which give him the courage and way to resist the machine and not have to compete, not have to conform to the hypocrisies of that society.

If Daddy wants Junior to stop being involved in drugs he had better realize what his side of the bargain is. Not only does have to stop leaning on his own pep pills, tranquilizers, sleeping pills, and martinis, but he has to restructure his whole society and eliminate all the false values he wants Junior to swallow—along with the pills. Then, to top that off, Daddy had better come across with a true awareness of God. He had better not only offer Junior a religion which can show him a natural way to live in the height of spirit but show Junior that Junior also can attain it. A big order. A staggering order. But I have a suspicion that Junior would gladly jump in and help, give up drugs or anything else, if he had even a hint that Dad was starting to build such a life and religion.

Anyone who thinks that the young are turning to drugs out of some kind of perversity or out of the pure and simple physical desire relevant to drink and other material indulgences of the past is wrong. Both consciously and subconsciously the young realize that their true life is not bound up in body and mind alone, that they live wherever their consciousness reaches and they are on a trip to find themselves in the most far-out distances of their awareness potential. When they are shown ways to explore themselves without drugs they are all too delighted to give them up, but not until.

Ways are coming. That's part of the ultimate revolution. And with those ways a new expression has been added to the "head" language. Experiencing a high without drugs is called doing a "natural."

The other day I was with a group when a girl came into the room with a big smile on her face, her head obviously in heaven. Someone commented, "What's she on?" and the answer came, "Nothing. She's doing a natural."

Almost everyone I know wants ultimately to do it natural. That's our birthright. We have within us, within our own soul and capacities, the spiritual muscles for having a natural high.

None of us should ever want to stay on an absolute continuous high. While we are still on the earth we need some lows to groove on in order to fuel the highs, but we will learn more and more how to arrive at a natural high and how to keep our heads there.

The Energy of Drugs

Any Morality of Grace for the new day is involved with maintaining contact rather than judging; so in order to understand how we lose contact we have to understand the energy of drugs.

As we know, every effect represents some kind of energy which in one way or the other keeps us in contact with ourselves and others. We know that alcohol and food primarily affect our mental and physical energies. After a night of heavy drinking or after overindulging in rich foods, we are down and heavy in body and mind. Our overindulgence has drawn too heavily on our mental and physical energies.

Well, drugs basically work on a different energy. That's both their appeal and their stumbling block. Drugs directly affect our spiritual or psychic energies. They appeal because they stimulate our spiritual forces. They make us aware of our spiritual potential and the highs of which man is capable. But certain of them can also overuse or drain those energies.

Sex and drugs have been the two things most feared by mankind because they involve man's two most vital energies. Sex involves the energy of life, representing creativity, material contact, and human love; drugs affect the energies involved in spirtuality and God contact, or the love of God.

An abundance and flow of the vital energies can lift us from material and mental bondage into the freedom of spirit; a lack or shortage of these energies leaves us earthbound and heavy.

Mystics have told us for centuries that there are certain key centers in the body, representing all levels of being from the most animal and primary to the ultimate and spiritual. They say that those who achieve completion in meditation contact all of these centers at various stages of the meditation. Now medical science has revealed that each of these centers corresponds to our various nerve centers and glands in the body.

The spiritual center, the mystics have always said, is between our eyes (the third eye). The Brahman, or spiritual caste, salutes this center by wearing a red dot on the forehead between the eyes.

This center corresponds to vital glands in our head which regulate our whole body and spirit. Drugs directly affect this center.

Drugs affect the glands which regulate our flow of adrenaline and similar glandular secretions such as the pineal and pituitary fluid.

They do it in various ways. For instance, marihuana stimulates the flow of adrenaline. LSD is a kind of imitation adrenaline which the regulatory forces in our body attack, trying to keep our adrenaline in check while our own adrenaline stimulates us into an unnaturally high state.

No matter how we are affected by drugs, it is actually our own adrenaline which turns us on. The kind of intoxication we feel when we experience joy, when we are stimulated by great art or spiritual exaltation, comes because, for some reason, those experiences have caused our glands to naturally produce something like a drug. For some reason, meditation results in a flow of adrenaline. In his book *The Varieties of Religious Experience*, William James wrote that all great saints or religious leaders had one thing in common—they were all highly adrenal people. In other words, they were turned on. They were high on the "natch," by turning on naturally.

At any rate, there seems to be some physical relation between the source of spirit, drugs, and glands, some bridge. We are just now beginning to understand these processes. Perhaps medical science will help us better understand the relation, but our job in the meantime is to avoid unintentional disconnects. Our job is to find out when and how we unintentionally use up too much of our energies in ways that cost us more than we want.

Protecting the Natural

I am not interested in defending or denouncing the use of drugs. I leave that task to those who are still living by a belief that effects are good or bad in themselves. But I am interested in protecting my ability to have a natural inner experience and in avoiding as many as possible of the downs which disconnect me from myself and others.

The danger is not in getting addicted by smoking marihuana or that smoking will lead to stronger drugs. If addiction is in one's consciousness, one can become addicted to anything from cigarettes to popcorn. There is danger whenever a person believes that any effect is good or that it has power in itself, no matter if it is food, drink, medicine, money, drugs, or anything else.

As I said, everything that we can interpret in third-dimensional terms is at the phenomenal level, is an effect. Food, drink, drugs, and even such esoteric phenomena as ESP and its identifiable results are all effects. They are not the real causes. The real cause is in the spirit of man which leads him to depend on effects. Whenever we become dependent on effects we may cut ourselves off from the source. The down or problem is not in the effect but in the disconnect we unintentionally bring by depending on the effects. Whenever we use effects, we can ask ourselves: Am I becoming dependent on this effect? If we are, then obviously we are being disconnected from the natural source of our own inner being.

Whenever we believe that any effect is good, we are bringing on a disconnect because we are neglecting the spirit. Actually, I should say that the only "power" is within man. A lot of effects are groovy. They are desirable to have. But in themselves they are neither good nor bad. If we think they are, we are back in the old mind-bound day ourselves. And the same applies to drugs. They are neither good nor bad; so we must watch that we don't think they in themselves are good any more than we should think they are bad.

When any effect is used in such a way that it keeps us from grooving on life it is a down. Whenever something is used because we want to avoid a down we may be cheating ourselves of the value of the down. Whenever an effect is used as a means of escaping from now it is being misused. When effects come into our lives as a result of the now, when they are a natural part of the present, then they fit into wholeness.

The point is that these principles fit the use of any effect. Any effect, if it is misused or if we become dependent on it, dissipates the energies of the self.

When people try dangerous stunts just for the fun of it, just for kicks, they are showing that they are not grooving on life. When people use so-called speed or pep pills—amphetamines, Methe-drine, Dexedrine, Benzedrine, and other stimulants which acceller-ate life all out of proportion, they are gobbling up life. For a brief period they may be seeing life from an exciting, jazzed-up view, but they had better get a lot out of it because they are sucking at the substance of life and in the end they have a corresponding down which might take days to pay for. These stimulants release adrena-line and other juices needed for the future. Tomorrow's juices are being used up today.

The down of using up tomorrow today is that boredom sets in. The person who has used up his tomorrow is disconnected from the ever-constant joy and excitement of life that is at his fingertips when his head is naturally high. He is bored because he has used up the juices which might have oiled the hours.

Each person has the potential of being the full blossom of God on earth. That's why we are here. We are like buds getting ready to bloom into flowers. Those of us who are here now are particu-larly lucky because this is the spring of mankind. A great mass blooming is about to take place. Perhaps a little fertilizing and pruning can help, but it's all going to happen in its own time, and that time is close at hand. We should encourage the blossom, but it would be foolish to pry the bud open by force.

We can grow to the place where we are able to experience an inner exaltation over a beautiful sunset, where we experience rap-ture at a work of art or a flower. We need these experiences in order to relate to the spiritual senses within us. We need these experi-ences before we can understand inner experiences of any kind. Anyone, young or old, who has not had spiritual experience from within himself in a natural way must always watch his balance because it may be hazardous for him to mess around with conscious-ness in areas which he has no past experience to relate to.

The high some people reach with a drug seems to be the ultimate to them because previously they were living in a depressed state and thought it was a normal condition for men. They didn't know the difference. It is fine that such people found life didn't have to be earthbound, but it would be a disconnect if they then failed to come to the realization that they don't need drugs to be high. It can be a natural state.

A great danger of forcing a high unnaturally is that it is like trying to reach the top without the underpinnings. When Plato said that man was in a cave looking at the shadows on the walls, thinking he was looking at life, he might have added that if man turned suddenly and looked at the sun without being prepared he could possibly blind himself. Or when Jesus said we must come by the sheepfold and that anyone who came another way was a thief and a robber, he might have meant that looking straight at the sun without being prepared could rob one of achieving the life of light as a natural and permanent experience.

Finally, drugs can present a very real problem in regard to meditation. Through using drugs, many people have attained an appetite for what they could achieve naturally, but the drug experience is so close to meditation that they become confused. The differences between being high through drugs and high through meditation are subtle. One who is familiar with drugs might keep trying to make the natural experience conform to the drug experience. It is sort of like trying to learn Spanish and Italian at the same time. They are so similar that one can get hopelessly confused. It has been my experience that a high on marihuana is like meditating through a screen. It's close but not the clear uninterrupted contact on the natural high. Also, drugs can even use the spiritual energies needed for meditation in such a way as to make meditation difficult if not impossible.

Changing Directions

It's one thing to explain how drugs and other effects can bring on disconnects that keep us from meditating or doing other things we'd like to do, but it's another matter to invent ways to reestablish contact once it has been broken. Our morality isn't complete unless it includes some basic principles we can follow in case we want to change habitual disconnects, large or small.

Of course, the most important and absolute way by which one can be reestablished and bring on a healing or change is through spiritual means, which we will touch on in the next chapters, but there are also ways the Man of Earth can set about changing his patterns through his personal actions.

The first, and most important, principle is that the *spirit* in which we are undertaking steps toward accomplishing a change must be up or high. There is no evil to fight, nothing to resist. We must be clear that we are not taking action negatively in order to change some evil, but rather that we act because we wish to experience some new or creative activity—for positive reasons.

The main reason that psychiatrists, ministers, and counselors have had unsatisfactory results in their attempts to change people's habits or sexual and drug patterns is because they have been unable to help people in ways that don't imply the presence of an evil which needed being overcome. They started with the premise or implication that the habit was bad and needed changing. In condemning it, they had the wrong spirit, or their patient did, and the condemnation just gave the habit more power. When guilt or condemnation is present, cures are impossible and the only thing left to do is to make a kind of prison warden out of the mind with which the person can try and discipline himself mentally.

It's a matter of self-love. As long as we are trying to change one of our habits, thinking it is evil, we cannot love ourselves and cannot change. When we realize, without condemnation, that we have some habit which causes us to miss out on other things we would like to experience, we can proceed and try to change the old habit out of the desire to experience something new rather than a desire to fight the old. This is a positive approach in a positive spirit. It's an up, not a down, approach.

Perhaps I am belaboring the point, but we *must* stay in love with ourselves at all times, which means that we must not see ourselves as being evil or separate from God because of some habit or pattern we have. We must not see a habit as a power apart from God. If we do, we are back in the old duality and we will never experience the new.

Say, for instance, that we have found a degree of inner experience by the use of drugs and now we would like to do it natural; we would now like to experience contact with God through meditation. Or perhaps we have known only homosexual relationships and we would like to experience a heterosexual relation. In both cases, we can desire the new experience, believing that it may be a high one, but we must not feel down about our old selves or condemn ourselves for not having been able to experience the natural in the past. The slate must be clean. We must look ahead, not backward. We must go into the new in just the right spirit with our will right, or there is no use trying at all.

Now because we have known sex or inner experiences in only one certain way in the past, we have to give ourselves time for that old conditioning to subside. We so greatly identify the experience as happening only one way that we have to give ourselves time to let it come another way. Again, we have to take that time in the right spirit, not grudgingly.

We have to let a certain amount of time pass because we all have need for highs or sexual contact, and often we have to let that appetite build up. For instance, in a rather oversimple way, we take ordinary things, such as hamburgers or bacon and eggs for granted, but anyone who has traveled abroad knows that after a year out of the country, he would give ten dollars for a hamburger or some bacon and eggs. So when a person wants to experience a new thing, he has to let himself build up a need or appetite.

A person who is trying to lovingly experience a heterosexual relationship should stay away from exclusively homosexual societies for a while and not encourage his thoughts on that line. Then after a time he should put himself in a position where there are members of the opposite sex, where the possibility of an association is present.

A person who uses drugs should build up his appetite for a spiritual experience by abstaining from having his extrasensual experiences through drugs. He should not keep his mind filled with thoughts about drugs, and he should frequent groups who are trying to do it "natural," for they help one another's desire to do it natural grow.

You see, the first experience that one has in meditation will probably not be as strong or obvious as the impact of a drug-induced experience. We have to really be hungry for that nonphenomenal experience, and then, when it gently starts, we have to spend possibly months making it grow and get stronger and stronger. It is rather like an athlete building a muscle over a matter of time with constant use and attention.

Finally, however, after we have abstained from the old and placed ourselves in surroundings conducive to the new, the consciousness takes over and the new experience can ignite. *But* the new experience will ignite only if the imagination is cooperative. Nothing succeeds, under grace, unless our will is positively directed and our imagination is cooperative. Whenever the will and the imagination are in conflict, the imagination will always win. The forms of our life are created out of our imagination, so there is no use in kidding ourselves. If we have a negative imagination, if we condition our imagination with paranoia or fear, if we have traces of condemnation in our imagination, we are locked into the old and can't experience or create a shiny new.

On the other hand, man can go anywhere his imagination can go, he can create anything his imagination can visualize, and he can experience any joy of life he wants—but he can do it only if he is not earthbound, if he is free from the belief in bad and good, and if he loves himself.

CHAPTER SIX

The Meditation Miracle

The mysteries of meditation and the efficacy of prayer have been dangled before the eyes of mankind, offering a sort of mystical pot of gold at the end of the spiritual rainbow, for too long a time. It is true that an inexplicable alchemy takes place when man experiences contact with the source within himself, but there is no need now for all the mumbo jumbo surrounding the attainment of this mystery. The techniques of how to meditate or pray have all too often been cloaked in a kind of snobbish exclusivity designed not only to whet man's appetite but also to blackmail him into signing away his individuality through joining a particular cult or accepting some one system over others as the authentic way of going about meditating.

It is up to us now, in the light of a new morality, to reveal the art of meditation as a present possibility for all. First, under grace, we must realize that there is no sin or evil to be overcome as a prelude to the experience of God. Second, there are some steps we can take, and if we take them in the right spirit, all the obstacles will dissolve.

In the past, the implication has always been that we must give up everything in order to experience God, that we must reject the material world. Naturally most people couldn't take that giant step because deep down inside they knew that the spirit of a true way couldn't include a rejection of life but rather must possess an all-encompassing love for life.

Obviously, a spiritual approach to meditation puts no one and nothing down. It knows that all mankind is one with God, so every man can realize his oneness. It is not exclusively for a person with one particular sex, nationality, or occupation, in one specific place or time. No fee need be paid, no human initiation is required, no lengthy discipline is demanded; in fact, spiritual contact is, as the Bible tells us, a "gift of God," and gifts are not earned by human effort. If we are not aware that each one of us already has this gift in his hands, it is because mankind has hidden it from us by mind-bending words; so let us find it.

In order to find it, we must answer a few questions. What actually is spiritual contact? How does it feel? What does it do? Why must we consciously make contact? What do prayer and meditation have to do with this contact? Then, how do we make contact? What are the techniques?

What is spiritual contact? To begin with, it is not all that mysterious. We have all felt it at one time or another to some degree or another, but often we haven't realized it. We haven't been aware of it, but we actually live by contact; it is our natural state. Since we haven't always consciously realized when we were in contact, we haven't taken conscious recourse to it in order to live life more fully and wholly.

Contact takes place any time we have ceased to be alone and cut off from the source of life, when our own separate personal vibration has been dropped and we step into rhythm with the vibration of life itself. Any time we are healed or recharged, strengthened or supplied, we are in contact.

How does it feel? It feels like being washed mentally, physically, or spiritually. It feels like exaltation. It feels like the bubbling up of joy within. It feels like being free of bodily limitations. That is why I say we all feel contact every time we experience delight over a work of art, a job well done, or a sport well played, or when we feel appreciation for man's accomplishments. We feel it every time we sense that we "belong." That's why man has such a desire to belong —it is hunger for the spiritual experience of oneness. Contact is the feeling of being recharged. It is the feeling of desireless love just for the sake of love itself. It is the feeling of light. It is the feeling of not only hearing a song but being the song. It is spiritual goose pimples.

What does it do? It cleans us. It reestablishes us when we are cut off. It chases away the cobwebs of the mind and spirit. It reveals to us where we have mistakenly got off the track. It heals us. It frees us to love. It ones us with the universe. All of that and vastly more.

Why must we consciously make contact if we are actually in contact all the time? We are in the morning of the day of grace when nothing need be rejected or put down. In order to live this new life, a conscious attainment of the contact experience is a necessity in order for us to live by guidelines which are not judgmental. In the old day, under law, man didn't make conscious contact with his true self. He let his mind live him; he set rules which were to apply day after day, telling him what was bad and what was good, so he would know how to act and react. All he had to do was to follow the laws. Now, under grace, he knows there is nothing on the face of creation which is always bad or always good. At each moment he must have some way of checking in with the truth in order to see if a person, place, or thing is in its right place, doing what it is "for." Making contact is how he checks in. It is the way the third-dimensional Man of Earth checks in with his own fourth-dimensional Man of God self. That check-in may take only a second, but it reveals the truth of life to such an extent that earth man can live for hours in a harmony with his material sense of life.

At a certain point the mind lets go and a oneness with all of life is felt. We are never quite the same after we have experienced this conscious contact or the inrush of energy and life. We still have to face all kinds of earthly problems, but never again are they quite the same—neither we nor the problems.

I have traveled a great deal, and for a number of years I thought I could imagine what it was like to go around the whole world. I had touched so many places in my sorties out from this country and back that simply by piecing together all of my impressions, I thought I knew what a full trip would be like. Once I finally made it all the way around in one trip, I felt surprisingly different. Now instead of my being in the world, the world was in *me.* I held it complete within my consciousness. Once we have had an experience, a conscious experience, which transcends our finite sense of self, we know what it feels like not to be in ourselves but to contain ourselves within ourselves.

Prayer and Meditation

Prayer and meditation are not the actual contact. They are just will or intent directed toward the contact. As such, they are really part of the third-dimensional sense of life. They, in themselves, are not spiritual but part of humanhood. They are part of our imagination in its attempt to create a contact through imaging it; they are a necessary step that the Man of Earth must take in order to arrive at the point of contact.

It is rather like a Boy Scout trying to make fire. He has to have a piece of flint and a piece of metal. He must keep them clean, dry, and in good condition if he expects to make fire. He hits the two together, maybe many times, in order to get the spark. The spark is the miracle, the contact. It is the flash point. Though it happens in the twinkling of an eye, it can start a whole fire.

Prayer and meditation are our tools. Prayer is mainly the intent or spirit in which we set out to make contact, and meditation is mainly the technique or physical means against which the intent is struck. When the two are in good shape, the contact is made and the fire of life is lighted.

Prayer is commonly associated with the Occident and Hebrew-Christianity; so is the love of materiality and the world. Symbolic or otherwise, the word made flesh or the importance of raising material standards has always been more strongly emphasized in the West. Western man's intent and his prayers have been directed toward personal and physical freedom. His mistake has been in getting a sense of right and wrong mixed in with his intent, but at least he hasn't rejected the world. The Orient has seen the danger in trying to make the world conform to man's ideas of good and bad; so the Orient has perfected meditation as the technique of dropping the personal sense and merging with God, but this in turn has often become a rejection of the world.

Now, however, we are in the new day when we realize we reach the fourth dimension both by merging so deeply in action that we become one with life and by refraining at other times from action, so that we stop perpetuating our own cut-off self. Prayer is spiritually directed action, and meditation is the cessation of action in order to contact spirit. Both are necessary.

In the Western world, we have distorted the right idea of prayer. We go to God asking for material things or for God to do our will, and instead of getting what we really want, we accomplish the opposite. We image duality and we create it. Anything we acknowledge, we demonstrate. In that respect, prayer is *acknowledgment* and vice versa. Even our *opinions are prayers* in that they create the flow of imagination and intent.

We quite naturally want harmony, and we know that it will be reestablished if we make contact, but the paradox is that we must go into prayer or meditation wanting *contact*, not *things.* The right kind of prayer intent is to meditate in an effort to find ourselves, not get something for ourselves, not get something, but know IT IS.

Prayer is a kind of knocking at the door of the collective unconscious. We have been so in the habit of taking thought in order to live our lives that we find we must change the direction. Prayer or contemplation is the act of changing the habit of *thinking* into the habit of *listening.* It is possible to listen to the "still small voice" within, to listen for a feeling. At any rate, prayer certainly isn't prayer unless it achieves a state beyond the thinking mind. Rather than taking thought, prayer is the process of freeing the mind. It means dropping all conditioned thought. It is *centering*—centering one's being in wholeness, not leaving it top-heavy in the mind.

Prayer is a kind of dying. Dying to the mind. As such, it is not a thing but a condition. It makes no difference how you get to that condition, but when you have let go of the sense of personal power, you have prayed.

One time I was working with an author friend of mine who was writing a play. Whenever he got stuck, he would call me in and we would discuss the problem. Sometimes we could solve the problem by using our intelligences, but at other times we were unable to find an answer. One day, a particularly difficult enigma was presented to us. After lengthy discussion, we gave up. We prayed; it was our intent to find help through prayer. Before long we both came to the awareness of: I of my own self can do nothing—and boom, the answer to our problem came through.

The next day another problem came in the course of the writing. Again I went to my friend's office and we discussed the situation awhile. When no answer came, we said, "All right, let's pray." Both of us thought we knew "how" to do it. We said, "I of my own self can do nothing." Then again, "I of my own self can do nothing." And again, "I of my own self can do nothing." And *nothing* happened. Finally, in desperation we gave up and felt: It doesn't work anymore—and then boom, once more the answer came through.

The point is, subconsciously we thought that by thinking: I of my own self can do nothing, we were creating the vacuum or getting out of our way, but we weren't. We were still thinking that there actually was something we could do. However, when we panicked and once more let go, we had arrived again at that open state where we could listen . . . could pray.

Listening is the key to prayer. It is the place where truth leaves the intellectual mind of reason and enters the soul where it is experienced.

This shifting makes a kind of spiritual change of chemistry in a person. Actually, the change affects even our material bodies. In the transition from larva to butterfly, the worm attaches itself to a limb, weaves a cocoon around itself, goes into a kind of meditative state, and changes its chemistry, resulting in a totally new body which emerges as a butterfly. Perhaps one day scientists will discover that some glandular action is brought on by prayer or meditation, altering our physical condition, but even if they do, I doubt that they will be able to explain how man can bring on this change purely from within himself.

The ability to bring on this change within ourselves is a new definition for *maturity.* The degree of our maturity is the degree of our ability to pray.

After all, maturity is gauged by our ability to handle in an unemotional and constructive fashion the pressures, the emergencies, and the problems we face. We can't do that unless we have found some way of keeping in touch with our oneness. No matter how we accomplish keeping inner contact, that way is prayer, because prayer is the ability to anchor within and withstand negative or confusing vibrations.

This kind of maturity has nothing to do with our age or type. When we do not react to upsetting or frustrating conditions, we are mature. Our ability to perform in a mature fashion shows we are able to pray.

Techniques of Meditation

Don't believe anyone who says he knows how to meditate. It is possible to individually find techniques which aid us in arriving at the flash point, but there isn't a successful meditation in which the person doesn't come to the point of giving up, of realizing he doesn't really know how to make it happen. When that point of human impossibility arrives, contact takes place. As long as we think we have the power to make it happen, we are still operating under the human mind and it doesn't happen. Ask anyone who has achieved the contact and he will admit that each time he experiences contact he feels for one split second that he is not going to get there this time, that he is helpless.

Our vibration or state of consciousness when we attempt to meditate may not be the same as the last time we meditated, so we must find different techniques to help us at different times. There is no one way.

Once when I was on a television program in California, the interviewer asked me, "How do you meditate or pray?" My answer sounded rather flippant at first. I replied, "Which me are you talking about?" I went on to explain that if someone woke me up at the crack of dawn, he might be met at the door by a rather disgruntled me, but if he knocked a couple of hours later, after I had got myself in running order, he would encounter a more friendly person. In the course of a single day, I am operating at a number of different vibrations. I must admit that I now operate at a higher level more of the time than I once did, but nevertheless, my level is not always the same.

Well, I have found for myself that I need different techniques at different times, depending on where I am at the moment. At times I am so greatly out of contact that I can't get any help from reading or from contemplating. I practically have to return to the old-fashioned prayers of my childhood religion, which taught me to get down on my bony knees and call on a God apart from myself. At times I must sort of blank out, take a nap, in order to release my fears. Then when I wake up I can start to read spiritual writings or practice other helps until I get my contact going.

At times I must go out into nature, walk by the water, or climb a mountain to make contact. Sometimes people are my prayer. If I communicate with my fellow man I can make contact. And certainly there are times when a kiss from a loved one is a prayer.

Also, at times I am living in such a sense of oneness that it would not only be redundant but a denial to sit down and meditate. It is there. I need only look over my shoulder, so to speak, and wink at it. If I were to deny it by thinking I had to become involved in some complicated ritual, I would be turning my back on the fact that IT IS.

To rely entirely on a system anyone else has devised might help for a time, but it does not include the freedom of infinite individuality. Using a ready-made system is rather like using an automatic camera. Today we have cameras on the market which eliminate a great number of the old hazards of photography. Just about anyone can take a pretty good picture. Automatic cameras certainly improve the quality or results of someone who has little talent for the use of a camera, but in turn, they limit one's true freedom. Automatic cameras are set up for the largest averages. In other words, most pictures are taken in midday; so the readings are calibrated for midday. Most pictures are taken of medium-contrast subjects, so the exposures are calibrated for medium contrast. To be really free, a photographer has to know how to make his own settings and adjust for pictures taken at any hour. The same applies to meditation. There is no set formula, no technique that fits for everyone at all times.

Before we go into specific aids, I would like to touch on some of the blocks or difficulties that most of us have felt in our attempts at meditation, particularly in our early days. At the beginning, we are often faced with the most primary kinds of self-consciousness. Our minds do everything they can to keep us from relaxing into meditation. If other people are around we feel personally embarrassed.

I remember the first time I tried to meditate in a group. We all closed our eyes and sat silently. The idea felt so preposterous to me that I had a difficult time keeping from giggling, my mind's way of keeping me self-conscious. After I got over that particular temptation, it never happened again, but I found that physical discomfort became a great handicap. The minute I tried to get quiet, my body became a beehive of feelings. I was aware of every bone and muscle. If I tried to force stillness on myself, I only managed to spend all my time thinking about my body.

The next trick my mind played on me was to bring on a tremendous desire to go to sleep. Sitting there with my eyes closed, I would find myself dozing off, and though I had every desire to go beyond my sense of self, I could do no more than concentrate on staying awake. Actually that was a good state because it always preceded a triumph over the mind. After the desire to sleep passed, my mind became fully alive, not with thoughts but with listening from within. Sometimes it was best to take a little nap rather than fight the mind by trying to stay awake. After the nap, my mind was quiet and contact was more easily attained.

There are also a few mental annoyances. The first is the belief that you don't have enough understanding to meditate. That, too, is a trick. You don't need understanding; you just need the desire or intent. The rest is up to God or the truth of one's self.

After you have experienced a bit in meditation, you may have psychic visions or experiences. They take over the mind by making you believe that it is necessary to have these experiences or that you haven't made contact without them. That, too, isn't true. You might very well hear sounds, see lights, or experience a number of manifestations, but those things are no more than signposts on the road. If you are tricked into believing that signs are necessary, you have forgotten the trip for the scenery.

Perhaps more people have been led astray by psychic phenomena than any other single thing. After an experience which manifests itself in some phenomenon, they proceed to become more involved in the phenomenon than in the contact. Look at the word "phenomenon." It tells the story. Anything to do with psychic phenomena which is explainable is of the phenomenal world. That makes it not a spiritual thing, but a phenomenal one.

I'm not putting down psychic phenomena, spiritualism, prophecy, or any of the other events usually associated with spiritual realization. I am just saying that they are not spiritual, as such; they are humanly identifiable and part of the third dimension. Perhaps they are a high form of the human, but they are human representations nevertheless, and if you get them confused with pure contact or the fourth dimension, you may find your meditations blocked and contact lost. You may find yourself back in the mental way of life.

If you experience voices, colors, or sounds, you can note the fact, you can appreciate that your contact produced the experience, but if you want to keep the intent of meditation pure, you must keep it focused on the experience of God, not psychic phenomena.

By the same token, you might find that after you start meditating, your physical system wants purer food or simpler eating habits. Perhaps you don't want to eat meat anymore. That is fine, but if your mind tricks you into believing that there is virtue in being a vegetarian or that eating meat has power over you, you are once more operating at the third-dimensional level of phenomena.

The greatest mental block to the experience has been perpetrated in the name of meditation itself. Because certain practitioners of meditation didn't realize that there is no evil, nothing to be condemned, and because they had no yardstick or Morality of Grace to measure with, their systems of meditation were based on the belief that there was a material world one had to overcome. They taught that we start in the gross world or the gross sense of life, then rise to the fine or subtle sense which goes beyond our limited sensual understanding, and finally experience the spiritual. In a way this is right, because we do go from our physical to a higher, super but not superior, sense. As long as we label the physical as being gross or evil or less good, we are back in the old duality. As long as we see the world as gross, we are again dropping out from being fully human. Any system of meditation which is based on the premise that the natural is gross is condemning the world and isn't a spiritual approach—the spirit is wrong.

Those who experience the subtle level for the first time are discovering a whole new world, and they can easily think it is the spiritual world. But actually it is a whole subtle material expansion. Those who, in the same way, experience the subtle world through LSD or mescaline might easily think they have discovered the spiritual world. In fact, they have understood in phenomenal terms, so they, too, have experienced an extension of the material world rather than the spiritual.

Then, too, a number of teachings, under the guise of meditation, say that we must use the mind to experience the subtle world until the mind arrives at the transcendent. But the danger is that the mind stays in control, and the real experience eludes us.

All of those teachings which advocate definite systems, which advocate disciplining the mind as though it is an enemy, which reject any activity or material thing, are still in the old day. They were right for their time and we can learn from them, but in this new day, we are our own teachers and we devise our own systems.

Some ABC's of Meditation

Meditation is like altering the direction of a wheel. It is shifting from the Man of Earth to the Man of God self. We must first slow the wheel down, then stop it, and then start it rolling the other direction. For what we might call silent or formal meditation in which we attempt to make contact by sitting quietly, turned within, to commune, there are some tips which might help. First, we slow the body down, then the mind and the senses.

In order to slow the body down and have the maximum control over it, sitting has always been considered the number one requirement for students of Zen and the Oriental religions which specialize in meditation. In the cross-legged sitting position called the lotus position, the body is rested yet the spine is straight; the nervous system is not pinched but is at its maximum of freedom.

Sitting on the floor isn't necessary, however. We in the West are not trained to sit cross-legged; so if we prefer we can sit in a chair which allows body freedom. The best chair is probably one with a straight back to keep us from hunching or unequally distributing our body weight, and allows us to rest our feet comfortably on the floor. It may be padded or at least not too hard and irregular. We can each try out various types of chairs until we find one in which we feel most comfortable and unaware of our bodies.

The belief that we absolutely must have a guru or teacher is also part of the old day. Most of us can find help from a teacher. Most often our fire is lighted from a teacher's fire, but, in fact, our consciousness is what has led us to the teacher in the first place. Our teacher is a creation of our own oneness with God, the God within our own being, only it is expressed outwardly as our teacher. If we believe that having a teacher is an absolute necessity, we have forgotten that we are in the new day when our oneness with God constitutes our oneness with all being. Our oneness with universal being is our true guru or teacher. A human teacher can only show us the aids he has found, but infinity can reveal helps which no single teacher knows.

It is a good idea to find a special quiet place for meditations in our homes. If we retreat day after day to some chair or corner in order to meditate, we find after a while that the place creates a kind of vibration or aura which helps us get quiet.

After sitting down in order to meditate, our first goal is, as the Orientals say, to *one-point* our minds and senses. That means we want to slow down the flow of thoughts and senses, create a kind of vacuum so the spirit can be felt.

Perhaps we have found that we are helped in our infinity of being if we create a kind of altar. This isn't necessary—in fact, it is harmful if we get superstitious about it—but it can be useful if our intent is not distorted. As we are making the voyage from the material sense to the spiritual sense, we may like to put a flower on our altar as the recognition of God's beauty expressed through nature. Perhaps we want to light a candle or incense. Actually, all of those things can have a dual purpose. They are dedications, and yet they are aids to one-pointing our senses.

We can even concentrate on the candle flame or the flower, or smell the incense, and in so doing, our whole being, body, mind, and spirit, is set about the task of letting go.

It is harder to one-point the mind than the senses, but even more necessary, and there are several ways we find help in that. Sometimes we can read from illumined writings which attract us, perhaps the Bible or Gita, until we feel an answering response within us. When we do, it is advisable to close the book and try to hold the feeling, not the thought, that the reading brought on. When it goes, we can open the book and repeat the experience. This reading and feeling can act like the starter on a motorboat. We try it and try it, and all of a sudden the motor sputters and starts. Then we don't need the book anymore; we are hearing from within.

Above all, we should not fight our thoughts in our attempts at meditation. Such struggling is like resisting evil: it only creates more thought. Thoughts don't really have power to keep us away from the contact. Just love them. Give them wings, and they will fly away. Without fighting, we can gently bring our mind back to the center, to the aim of our activity.

Frequently people say, "I can't meditate because I can't stop thinking." But thoughts don't have power. Thinking isn't the problem. The problem is when we think thinking is a handicap and try to resist thinking as though it is an evil. The spirit of resistance is what gets in their way.

Though we don't fight the mind, there are some helps we can use in returning the mind to center. One of these is the Hindu technique of the use of the *mantra.* A mantra is a word or phrase on which we can concentrate in order to bring ourselves into line with the vibration of being. The Christian religion contains many mantralike statements, such as, "Thy grace is sufficient for me in all things," or, "I have come that ye might be fulfilled," or even the Hail Mary's of the Catholic Church. When we find our mind wandering, we can gently direct it by returning to a contemplation of our mantra.

Above all, we are not trying to bludgeon the mind out of existence. We want to blank the mind so it can be used by the spirit, but we want it alive and free.

In the past a teacher gave his student a mantra designed for the student's present state of consciousness. The idea was that when the student reached a higher state, a more advanced mantra would be given to him. Initiation only meant that the guru meditated with the student, sensed what vibration the student was at, and gave him a mantra to fit. If the student was at a very personal or restless vibration, his mantra would fit that situation.

The theory was, under law, that if the student meditated with a mantra which was beyond his comprehension, his ego would get involved and he would be harmed or misled. In a sense that is true. If a person can't help but see himself in terms of his own ego, he can't meditate on his oneness with God without thinking that he, in his human identity, is God.

Perhaps a beginning student was told to meditate on some simple word like "peace" to slow down his fears. When that had been attained he was told to meditate on "not this, not this, but thou, thou," as a way of shifting from the human sense to God identification. Eventually he would be ready to meditate on "I am and God is." Often a student was told to meditate on a word without real or human meaning in order to lift the mind beyond conditioned thought—as the word "OM" is used by the Hindu, and "IS" is used by the Occidental.

IS, just is or isness, has nothing the mind can hang on to, so it is easy to go beyond thought to feeling. Everyone needs such an indefinable word at one time or another.

Finally, we can arrive at the absolute. We can contemplate the word "I," the pure oneness within. But at that time we should have reached the state where the *I-ness* is comprehended without its being mixed up with personal identification.

As I said before, we go to meditation at different times in different states of consciousness; so no single mantra is always the right one. It is up to us, under our new morality, to sense what state of awareness we are in and use whatever mantra works for us at that time. If we get quiet and listen, our spirit will tell us our mantra.

In place of one set mantra we can begin by contemplating whatever truths come into our mind. Perhaps Bible quotations will pop to our attention. If we mull them, listen to them, contemplate them, we may begin to feel a sense of silence within or we may find light flooding our being. One quote may flow into another and another until we realize that it isn't our mind bringing them forth, but rather that they come from the collective unconscious, or God. Don't forget, man's words mean little, but God's words are "swift and sharp as a sword." God's words can move the world, and they slip into contemplation before we know it. But they do it in silence, the silence within. Contemplation can be a help, but only if it leads to silence.

Finally, after we have yielded our bodies, after we have stilled our senses, after we have concentrated our minds so intensely as to recede from externals into emotional stillness, after we have contemplated truth until we reach silence, we experience the flash point. Perhaps we feel an inner "click," a deep sigh that goes right to our toes, perhaps an inner sense of light, even a bubbling up of joy. It takes only a split second. It is seldom more than the most brief of moments. But in that moment, God is on the field and we are merged into life itself. We feel serenity and exaltation of body and spirit.

When, Where, and After Contact

Once we have recognized contact, everything else falls into place. After making contact we can take those problems we have put aside—in order to keep from going into meditation with human desires—and hold them up to the light of our inner contact. Now we can let our minds drift across our life like a radar over a radarscope. When a person, place, or thing pops into our consciousness, we measure it against the release we have just had and receive the guidance we can be given from within. We don't hoard the experience; we don't drop out by trying to keep on perpetuating the feeling indefinitely.

Even here some people have lost the way. They have experienced the joy of a contact in meditation but believed that there was some virtue in long meditations. There isn't. Overlong meditation sessions are even self-indulgent. They are similar to getting "stoned" on taking too much drugs.

The object of meditation is to receive the light and then come back into the world to make it a more light-filled place. I know it is tempting to want to stay in that peace; it is often hard to return to the active world; but meditation for the sake of personal enjoyment alone is a disconnect with the world and our responsibility to our fellow man. It is far better to make the contact many times in a day than to sit for long times in one stretch.

There are special times for meditation, but any time is the right time. It is advisable to set aside a time at the beginning of each day in order to get programmed for the day, to get the right vibration started, and it is often good to meditate before going to bed at night. An evening meditation sort of flushes out the day, rejects the unintentional irritants one has taken on by third-dimensional living. Then the night is more restful and we find we even need less sleep. But any time is the right time.

During the course of a day, we may feel what I call pulls or pressures. These are signs to us that we need to get in step. Most of us know that if we get started on the wrong foot we may stay out of step until we change our vibration. Meditation is how we do it.

Even if we are off in the business world, when we feel a pull or heaviness we can always find a private corner or close our office door for a moment of meditation. When we don't feel a pull or pressure, there is probably no need at the moment to meditate unless we wish to renew the contact for the sheer joy of it.

The time it takes for meditation varies. Sometimes it happens in a moment. It may take an hour to make the contact. There is no law. Each must come to know himself. Each must come to know what it feels like to contact God as personally as he knows what it feels like to contact the one he loves.

CHAPTER SEVEN

The Healing Spirit

The subject of healing has been the hot potato of the Christian message, or any spiritual message, for that matter. It can't be ignored, and yet no one has known how to handle it. After the early years of Christianity, when the Christian message was codified and placed under law, the spirit of grace left, and with it went the ability to heal. The secrets of healing were still buried there, but man was blinded to them. From then on, healing became a cruel subject. On one hand, healing was held out as a possibility which was bound up in the spiritual life. On the other hand, people's hopes were constantly dashed to the ground by man's inability to bring healing about.

In the past few years, the possibility of spiritual healing has been brought out again because we are on the verge of the spiritual day and healing is an integral part of the life lived by grace. But even now there is a great deal of confusion about healing, for this is a time of transition.

Most reasonable people shy away from the whole subject of spiritual healing. I did. I had come from a family of physicians. The doctors in my family were sometimes called in too late to save the failures of those who tried to force healings with their minds or blind faith, but didn't know what they were doing. Naturally we thought spiritual healers were the devil's handmaids.

I also wanted desperately to rise beyond having to judge the world as bad or good, sick or well. I wanted to love the world, not judge it, not say, "O.K., I'll love you when you are better, more healthy, more wealthy, more successful."

I couldn't stomach any more personal guilt, and if I had to consider sickness as failure and health as success, then I would be back in the old trap of not being able to love myself whenever I was sick.

Most important of all I felt I had to believe in God in order to have an inner anchor, but I was too intelligent to believe that God could be God if there were any other power apart from God; and if I equated God with healing, I would have to believe that either God failed where sickness was concerned or else God was some kind of a monster who allowed sickness to take place unless people said the right words or thought the right thoughts.

The whole subject smelled of hypocrisy, of man's ego, of wishful thinking, of blind faith, of people's disappointments which in turn made them lose faith in the true source within themselves. I wanted none of it. So when I came into a growing awareness of what it meant to live by spirit, I rather resented the intrusion of the subject of healing. I didn't want to cloud up the water. Then, little by little, I couldn't help but notice how my own health began to improve as I progressed on my search. Sometimes patterns of ill health were mysteriously replaced by illogically quick recovery. Other illnesses left without the help of medication. I wasn't just healed physically. All kinds of personal problems involving a need for money and human relations seemed to dissolve as a result of some kind of spiritual influence. I had to face the reality of spiritual healing. And with having to face it, I had to face my own responsibility toward healing both myself and others.

Nobody in his right mind wants to set himself up as a healer. First of all, nobody knows how to heal. Even a doctor knows that he can prescribe medication but he can't actually produce healing, any more than a mother can raise a fingernail on her child. The healing process may operate by using man as an instrument, but none of us knows any more how to heal than we do how to meditate or know God.

Besides being an impossibility, healing also presents a personal danger. Any time man sets himself up as either a healer or a spiritual teacher, he puts himself in a position where eventually he assumes a kind of personal superiority—he has the message the public needs, or he has the power to help God out. Unless those who proclaim themselves as healers are very solidly anchored in spirit, before long they begin to believe that they have power of themselves.

The desire to heal or teach tempts one to forget that the kingdom of heaven is already here. The temptation to change the world is a put-down of the world. When a person begins to think of himself as a healer, he begins to cut himself off from the source. Little by little his effectiveness decreases. Healing is effective because of man's capacity to break the illusion of separateness by experiencing that actuallly there is no evil to fight. If one calls himself a healer he has to live up to the title, so an unsuccessful healer has to start compromising, falling back on law, and blaming others for his failure. It's a title to avoid.

But, and this is an important *but* to understand, the higher we go in consciousness, the more we experience our own oneness, the more others are attracted to us for help. Others sense a vibration, a harmonizing, cleansing, or healing vibration. Most often those who come around a person who has achieved some awareness of the life lived by grace don't even know what they come for; they just know they want to be near that person. Often they start asking for help in little, indirect ways. They may not say, "Pray for me," or, "Heal me," but they say, "I feel better after I have been with you," "I get a lift from you," "There's something about you that helps me and makes my problems go away"—and that's the same as asking for help.

Then it is the response-ability of the person who has the lifted consciousness to give his help, for giving his help is giving his self. He has to for purely selfish reason: he has to be alive and living. He has to give in order to be blessed with the life force which makes him so spiritually attractive to others. But mostly, he has to lift and heal others because he knows that they are all connected to him; they are all projections of his own self; they have all come into his consciousness and are therefore a part of himself just as his own hands and feet are connected to him.

Even those to whom none are turning for help must start healing. After all, we get by our giving. If we wish to be made whole ourselves, we start making others whole. We can begin in the simplest of ways. We don't even need to let anyone know, but every time an appearance of inharmony or disconnect appears in the lives of those around us, we can begin by seeing through the appearance to the truth.

Finally, however, and this sounds as if I am contradicting my statement that no one should set himself up as a healer, we must make a commitment to others by letting them know we are willing to do what we can. We don't have to say, "I will heal you," in a manner which mistakes the *I* for the ego, but we must let our family of mankind know that we are all linked together and that we are ready to offer our consciousness at any time it is wanted.

It is easy just to say, "I'll pray for you." But if the word "pray" is too ickey with old morality, we can say, "Any time you want to use some of my up, my contact, my juice, it is all yours." That's saying: I'll pray for you. Anytime we let others know we are going to go off somewhere quiet and release their problems for them— which is easier for us to do than it is for them because they are more personally involved—we are saying: I will pray for you. When we get over judging and can experience inner harmony, we are praying for them, we are healing them.

Now, this has nothing to do with one person's being more spiritual than the other. It doesn't mean one person knows more about healing than another. There isn't a person who has read this

book, or any of the New Testament for that matter, who doesn't
know enough to heal.

It's this: Perhaps one day I am down and you are not. I can say
to you, "Give me a zap." And you can, because you are up that
moment. My asking constitutes a link. On another day, you might
be down and I am not; so you say to me, "Say, I'm wrecked today,
give me some help." And this time I help the healing along.

Meditation and healing go hand in hand. When we meditate and
make contact, invariably more wholeness manifests itself. We
might say that meditation is *how* and healing is *what*. The paradox
is that we cannot meditate with any purpose in mind other than the
purpose of letting go and experiencing the allness of life. However,
when that allness is experienced in its absolute or fourth-dimensional sense, we become more free and whole at the personal level.

When we feel a pull, a down vibration, we recognize it as the
signal to go reestablish our wholeness by checking in with our God
self. In other words, we know it's time to heal ourselves, and when
we heal ourselves, we are contributing to the healing of all others.
As a matter of fact, when we feel a pull, it can be for one of three
reasons: Something of a purely personal disturbance or "down" is
looming on our horizon. Someone in our family to whom we are
hooked up is having a negative experience which we sense by our
oneness with him. Something of a universal nature is affecting the
whole family of mankind.

No matter which situation caused the pull, there is one basic
thing we have to do—go back to center and reestablish contact with
the truth of being. If we go beyond the temptation to believe in bad
and good, realize God is the only power, and free ourselves of any
judgment, grace begins to manifest itself. We have removed ourselves from law. Wholeness and freedom are established. A healing
has taken place.

Alas, the next time a pull comes, or the next time we are presented with a problem, we know that healing can take place, so it
is all the more difficult to keep from trying to judge. It's hard to

keep from thinking: That situation is bad—I better heal it. But when we want to change appearances we have slipped back into the old way of living where we judged by bad and good. It's tricky.

Sure, healing is a tricky business. But we are safe as long as we remember one thing, as long as we keep this one thought indelibly printed on our foreheads: NO MAN CAN HEAL. The only thing that heals is the breakthrough from the third dimension to an experience of the fourth dimension. The only thing that brings harmony is the ray of light that is let in when a consciousness rises to that level, and no man can do that out of personal will or human knowledge, out of personal power or desire. So remember: I can't heal. And then go heal.

Pitfalls

It is up to us to get clear on just what spiritual healing is in order to avoid the pitfalls. Healing means a reestablishing, returning to wholeness, harmonizing, and fulfilling. It doesn't have to be just a physical healing. Any time we return to wholeness in supplying our material needs, our creative needs, or in making our human relations whole, we are healing.

The words *heal, whole,* and *holy* all come from the same root, an Old English word, *hel,* meaning *complete.* When we heal, we make whole, and a whole man is a holy man. Obviously a holy man is one who is operating in complete balance between his earth self and his God self. A holy man is one who has neither dropped out of the world nor turned his back on the material world.

How we judge holiness in the new day? Simple. We don't! Nothing is holy, and nothing is unholy. Everything we see with our eyes is a finite third-dimensional view, no matter how favorable or unfavorable it appears. Absolutely everything is reaching out to holiness, to becoming more infinite and whole, but no thing and no one seen in terms of the third dimension is holy, whole, or completely healthy. It is up to us to *experience* holiness, not look for it with our eyes and minds.

We don't try to make third-dimensional man holy or whole. We don't try to change anything we see at the phenomenal level. We don't try to bring God into the third-dimensional level; rather, we take man up to God. We recognize the problem, but then we put it aside and experience the universal oneness. As long as we are making treatments or trying to know truths about a person, place, or thing, we are at the mental level and not at the spiritual.

The greatest handicap to spiritual healing is man's good intentions. The more man wants to heal and the more he believes in bad and good, the more tightly he locks himself under law. God already is, perfection already is, wholeness already is. Our job is to experience it, not try to make it true.

We need know only two things in order to heal: One, *that* God is—that there is a ground of all being, a universal wholeness, an ultimate truth, and that all living being is contained in that all-embracing isness. Two, *what* God is—one power against which all beliefs in evil or separateness disappear. That's all we need to know with our minds. The trick is the experiencing of it, but if it is experienced, then discord gives way to harmony and suddenly what appeared destructive is revealed as part of growth or it just plain dissolves.

One of the saddest things I have witnessed has been churches or groups who were conducting healing services in which, instead of healing, people were doing the exact opposite. No matter how conscientious and well intended the participants were, by not knowing what they were about, they were making matters more difficult. Rather than dissolving the negative into oneness, they were trying to evoke some power over the negative and were instead giving it power. By seeing the people they were trying to help as sick and unfortunate people, the healers were believing in the finite interpretations of the people they wanted to help and were not establishing them with their true identity as one with God.

Sometimes prayer groups use a system in which the members

one after another say the name of someone they want the group to pray for. That could be all right if the member didn't say what the claim or down was. When he says, "Pray for Mary who is having a difficult pregnancy," or, "Pray for John who is in trouble with drugs," he succeeds only in causing everyone in the room to visualize a Mary with a difficult pregnancy or a John who can be harmed by drugs. If anything helps create the situation, it is the imagings of those in the room. In turn, if the names alone are given without the problem being stated, those who want to heal don't set their imaginations to work creating the problem. Without visualizing the problem, the group thinks: That person is no different from any of us. We are all whole and one in our spiritual identity. If the group then releases the problem, not to a blind God but to the truth, an experience takes place. The vibration is lifted and the person being prayed for is freed from the problem.

Most of those practices called spiritual healings are not really spiritual; they are mental. We can test whether a practice is mental or spiritual by seeing if it includes taking a human ill or discomfort into the meditation or thought, if it implies that health is better than ill health. As long as a healing technique implies that the other person has to do something—for example, think good thoughts, reform, or stop sinning—it is dealing at the moral level and has nothing to do with pure spirit.

All the ills man has are like masks one wears at a party. There are hundreds of different masks: the mask of sickness, the mask of poverty, the mask of divorce, the mask of failure. But they all cover one face. That face is a belief in a power apart from God. A spiritual healer knows that the masks are only visible projections of the one problem: a sense of separation from God. He doesn't try to fight the masks. He sees them, then he goes beyond them to the cause. Any teaching that says it is necessary to label the masks is in the mental and not the spiritual.

A spiritual healer deals with a misapprehension of reality, not colds, cancers, drug addiction, stealing, cruelty, or war. A spiritual healer doesn't try to erase the snakes from the wall when a man is undergoing d.t.'s; he doesn't try to fight the goblins that appear in a nightmare. Rather, he sobers up the person and wakes him from the dream. When awake, the person is whole once more.

Practical Steps

An Episcopalian minister friend and I were talking about healing. He told me how he was called by one of his church families to go sit at the bedside of a man who was dying in the hospital. As he sat there alone in the room beside the man who was in a coma, he tried to pray, as the family had requested. He was overwhelmed with his helplessness and the realization that there wasn't any way he could make God work. In his anguish, he really experienced: I of my own self can do nothing, and to his amazement, before long, the man came out of his coma and in a few days was well. My friend was confused because he didn't know how it had happened. He wasn't aware that by coming to the realization that nothing could be done third-dimensionally, he was lifted beyond bad and good into the spirit, and when the ray of light broke into this level, a healing took place. Actually, he had stopped thinking about the man and had healed himself.

The first step in a practical approach to being an instrument for healing is to realize that we really only heal ourselves. When we heal ourselves of a belief in a power apart from God, the picture we have in our own consciousness changes.

When a person has asked for help, that is all he needs to do, and that is all we need from him. He has entered our consciousness by his request for help. It sounds odd, but our job is to realize that the person doesn't need help. Strangely enough, as with good intentions, the best healers are those who seem the most impersonal, who react least to negative appearances. Perhaps this isn't really strange. Look at the strongest person you know, the one to whom you turn for help in a time of trouble, and you will invariably see that he is a person who won't react violently or emotionally when you tell him your problem. Such persons are healers. They realize God is still on the field, no matter what appearances testify.

Under grace, the degree of man's faith is not what he says he believes; it is the degree to which he reacts.

For instance, one man is told his house is on fire. He immediately goes into a panic, starts running frantically and calling for help. You know by his actions that he is not very secure within, that he thinks his good is bound up in his house, that he doesn't believe in his power to make another house if that one burns.

Another man is told his house is on fire. He almost jokingly says, "Well, let's see what we can do about it. If we can't put it out, maybe we can roast some marshmallows." You know that this man does not base his life on externals, that he isn't disconnected from the source of life.

Now, what do we do if someone telephones us for help? First we let the caller tell us the trouble so he can get it off his chest and believe that help is on the way. But it would actually be better if he said no more than "I need help." We know that no matter what the problem is, it is just a belief in a power of evil, so what we are curing is the belief. If we do let him tell the problem, we let him tell it only once and not repeat himself over and over, for that just deepens it. We should limit the telephone call as much as possible so we can immediately get release. We assure the caller, "I'll be with you," and then get off the line.

It is often best to keep contact by telling the person to call the next day or in an hour if he is in pain. At any rate, as long as he wants help, we should let him know we are keeping contact.

Then we set about healing ourself. If we are in public, we can retire to our own quarters or a quiet spot. Then we open ourself for the experience of release. Perhaps we have to use a mantra or do some positive thinking in order to get our mind quiet, but our goal is not to change anything; it is in experiencing our own contact with true being. It may take a couple of minutes; it may take hours. If it takes a long time before we really feel a release, perhaps we have to try for a while, break off, and try again later, but we have the responsibility to keep at it until we feel our own rightness. That's all we can do.

Free will enters here. We must have the will to remember the highest truths we know and reexperience what we know. We need to have the will to heal our own belief that there is someone needing healing.

After we have felt our release, that is all we can do. We get up and go about our business. If the problem later pops up again in our consciousness, we must again experience our freedom and repeat the process over and over every time the problem comes into our mind. If the troubled person calls again and still wants help, we sit down once more to check in with reality, but if we feel that all has been taken care of, we would be denying the truth and assuming that we personally had power if we kept on trying.

A man once called me for help, saying he had a backache. I said I would stand by. I went to my room. It took me half an hour to release my belief that I had to help him, that evil was on the field. At any rate, I got my release and went about my business. The next day he called again and said, "It's worse." I said I would continue my work and hung up. Once more I went to my room to check in with the spirit, but right away I had the feeling that there was nothing for me to do. Well, the next day he called again. "It's worse. I can't sleep and my whole back aches now." I asked if he wanted me to continue and he said he did. Once more I checked in, and once more I didn't feel that I had anything to do. My mind kind of wanted to go on thinking something or trying in some way, but I knew I couldn't heal that way, that all I could do was keep myself in tune, so I went about my life.

The next morning, the man called. He said, "Well, that beats all. Last night I got mad. I said, 'That guy isn't going to help me. Nothing is.' And I gave up. Then out of the blue the pain went away and I was free." When he stopped looking for me to heal him, when he stopped trying to use mental power, he got his healing.

Actually, the healing took place the first day. That is why I didn't feel any more pull. But the backache was there in order to help the man grow, and when he learned his lesson of growing, it left. The healing was the spiritual principle he learned, not the relief of a backache.

Under grace we are interested in the expansion of consciousness, in the growth of wholeness, not in patching up bodies or empty purses. Jesus showed us that. He actually healed very few people. He wasn't interested in just making the world a more comfortable place. He was interested in showing mankind its freedom, and at times, by examples of physical healing, he showed that we have in consciousness that which can free mankind. But you will notice he healed only those who reached out to him, those who touched him mentally or physically. Once they had touched him, they had linked up with his consciousness, they were in a position to see his truth work, and they were pulled into his wholeness.

When the man at the well asked for healing, Jesus made no emotional or human reaction at all. He simply said, "What's to hinder you? Take up your bed and walk." Jesus was so high that he didn't even see the human illusion of sickness! He saw the true freedom in the man. And by seeing it, the man was lifted into it, lifted right up onto his feet.

Spiritual healing has nothing to do with time or space. A person wanting help can be in Timbuktu; it makes no difference. If he makes contact either by telephoning or by writing, or even by sending out mental telegrams, he is joined up into the oneness and the work is done.

Our job is to stay in as high a state of consciousness as we can at all times. The more people are looking to us for help, the more responsibility we have to stay high and make contact as often as possible. When there are those who are not even making recognizable contact but who are reaching out to us in their thoughts, we may not know it, so we have to keep ourselves open. If we feel pulls, someone may be reaching out to us; so we simply recognize that we have to go within and release whatever is causing the pull.

The highest healing state is the one in which a person doesn't even know he is healing, where his presence alone heals, where he leaves a trail of lifted people behind him just by the lifting power of his vibration.

That is where we will all be one day. One day, when the light has finally chased away all belief in bad and good, we will need no healers and no teachers. All will be hooked together in a lifting vibration, and when one member of the family of mankind starts to lag, the other members will support him just by their presence.

Neither Do I Condemn Thee

The hardest condition to heal is one in which the healer is personally involved. We might find that many, many others reach out to us and that light is brought into their lives, but when it comes to helping the members of our own family, it isn't as easy. That's natural and has nothing to do with success or failure.

Our family is part of our own picture. A picture can't jump out of its frame and turn around and see itself. It is easy to see the truth about someone else's family because they are not part of our own picture. When we are personally involved, we have two things to do: One, we give up our own personal responsibility by reaching out for help from others who we feel are good vibrations. Two, we listen within to see if our own problem isn't part of our growth.

Our problem might be the breaking up of old forms so that new ones can come forth. If we halt the apparent disruption, we might be halting progress or growth. But if the disruption is a real disconnect brought on by our ignorance, then it can indeed be healed and lifted. Whether it is our own problem or that of someone who has reached out to us, we must not judge in terms of human good or change involving personal desire.

The minute we judge, the minute we look for results, we are back in the world of law. The minute we are in law, we start condemning some as good and others as bad. Then when we see people we know who are mixed up and operating under ignorance, we judge them and cannot heal them.

Whenever we let the slightest judgment enter, whenever we let the slightest feeling of superiority enter, whenever we see those who reach out to us in terms of their failure, we are condemning them, not loving them. Before Jesus healed, he said, "Neither do I condemn thee." That is our motto.

When we look to the life of Jesus for further tips on the spiritual life, or a morality based on grace, we find that he kept telling his followers that they should go heal. The disciples were actually the first revolutionary recruits trying to live by a new morality, and they made the same mistakes we do. They went out and found that there was indeed something in their consciousness which made healings possible. Then they came running back to Jesus all puffed up by their accomplishment. But he called a quick halt. He said, in effect: Now wait a minute; rejoice only that your names are written in heaven.

What is heaven? It is the pure state of wholeness. Heaven is not some place off in the distance. It is right at the spot where we are when we realize our wholeness. The kingdom of heaven is within because our wholeness is within. As long as we stay in contact with our wholeness, we are welcome to the joy of life itself. That's why we are on the verge of the most joy-filled day the world has ever seen, as man more and more actually realizes his wholeness. As that day grows into fullness, we will have heaven on earth, literally. The world will become a holy place.

The holy place is the holy level of consciousness. We are at the doorway of that place. My friend and teacher, Joel Goldsmith, in his book *The Art of Spiritual Healing*, wrote: "I stand at the doorway of my consciousness, permitting nothing of a discordant nature to enter, maintaining it in its purity as that place through which God flows to all the world. All who enter my spiritual household, my temple, find therein the peace and joy which become the substance of their being, their bodies, or their pocket-books. This God-consciousness envelops them, governs and sustains them, and reveals this truth as the truth of their own individual being, so that they, in their turn, become a law not only to themselves, but to all who look to them for help."

CHAPTER EIGHT

The Ultimate Trip

My life is an adventure. In terms of my name and my identity, it is a journey into time and space. In terms of consciousness, it is an endless journey into infinity. At best, it is a glorious trip into which I take my whole self.

From day to day, I have taken many side trips. At one point, I made material success my trip. At another time, the acquirement of human knowledge was my trip. Sometimes making the world a more beautiful place has been my trip, and sometimes I have been on a people trip.

For a while I made sex my trip. For a time I was on a self-indulgent trip. Once I made the rejection of life itself my trip.

Who is to judge the value or harm of any of my trips? Eventually, and along with all the other trips, as I journeyed the whole map of human existence, I was led to the *ultimate trip.*

The ultimate trip is the journey into spirit. Once I had firmly set my foot on the ultimate trip, all else seemed pale and limited, for all other trips were only facets of the ultimate trip.

Through the ultimate trip I found my love, my purpose, and my life. The ultimate trip is a life lived by grace. It is the life of life and the all of all. It is beyond the judging of all other trips. It does not proselytize. It does not try to lure others into its path by condemning other trips. It simply says, "Let your own light so shine before men that they might see your good works." All mankind is drawn to the light illuminating the ultimate trip.

How do I know when I am on the ultimate trip? Simple. I know because I know what I place at the center of my life. Whatever I place at the center is my trip. I know I do not place money at the center, so I am not on a money trip. I know I do not place work at the center of my life, so I am not on a work trip. I know I do not place sex at the center, so I am not on a sex trip. I know that food, drink, or drugs are not at the center. I know I do not think about them or relate everything to them, and whatever I place at the center is that which I relate to. Whatever I relate to is the morning star which guides the ship of my life.

My morning star, the ultimate of ultimates to which I relate, can only be one thing—GOD. God is the ultimate trip. I place God at the center.

Now I know my heart has always yearned for God. All the other trips have been paths leading to the ultimate trip. Having once tasted an experience of God, everything else continues to exist but it exists as a shadow receiving its light from the light of God.

I have found the pearl of great price, and I am willing to sell all I have to buy it. I am willing to offer up my own individual self, the most valuable thing I have, for the ultimate trip. That's the final price.

By paying this price, I have found out a wonderful thing to behold—*I am all that God is.* I am a marvelous thing. I have access to all the heavenly riches. I am beauty and I am love.

Am I willing now to turn around and give even that up? I must, if I want to take the ultimate trip, because the ultimate trip transcends all separateness and merges me into God itself. Like the prodigal son, I came out from God and now I want to return, I want to complete the journey, I want to make the round trip back into the totality of my beingness from which I came. What must I do to make this last step on the trip?

I must walk the last mile alone. That means that I cannot walk it with the help of any material person, place, or thing. I cannot lean on a teaching, a teacher, a pill, or any of my personal accomplishments.

Finally, after I have been through all the other trips from which the collective human soul has grown, I stand naked of soul. Then at last I can see an object attracting all soul. In order to lose my final traces of separateness, I must recognize a center at once a part of me and yet apart from me. That is God. God is the center of attraction.

Only by putting God at the center can I experience it and finally merge into it. I must put something bigger than my own consciousness at the center, for just as the leaf has all of the vine within it, the vine is more than the leaf. Just as every cell or organ of my body has a life and activity of its own, I am more than all the parts. So, just as all of my fellow men are cells making up the whole of God, God is both all of us and more than any of us.

When I put God at the center, I can experience it and finally merge into it as others have done. Others before me have washed the world with the light shed from their ultimate trip, and each one of them said, "I and the father are one, but the father is greater than I." They showed the world by their example that it is possible for me, too—that I have the same potential.

When I realize that Jesus, Buddha, Mohammed, and Rama Krishna proved that man could make the ultimate trip, I know they did it for me because by making the trip themselves they showed me that I can make it. I love them for that.

To realize the very presence of Jesus Christ is to experience him as a living reality. To experience the Christ myself is to experience the possibility of that spiritual evolution which is taking place within me. The love of Jesus Christ is the love of the possibility, the recognition of the possibility.

I must recognize him, and recognizing the possibility in him is the bridge that lifts me totally into his very being and into the total of God. The evolved accomplished soul of Jesus fills me when I evolve into his fullness, when I accomplish his trip. It is at once me and apart from me, and I can say, as Paul did, "I live, yet not I, but Christ in me." Now I and the Father are one.

Now when I pray, it is not I who prays; it is the God within me who prays. My prayer is not my prayer, but it is God praying ME:

I in the midst of the world feed it, clothe it, and house it. I in the midst of you have never been limited. I in the midst of you provide everything necessary to you at all times, for I am not dependent on man who appears separate from me.

I am neither male nor female. I am the *I* which is in all mankind. I am the universal, supreme, divine, true identity of all, no matter what color, race, size, or shape.

I am all. I am the invisible presence in all, showing forth as the many forms of myself. I am the invisible presence which travels through life beside me. I am the life of friend or foe.

I have come that I might have life and that I might have it more abundantly. I have come to fulfill myself, and as you are I, I am fulfilling you when you put me at the center. Now cease from depending on man for your good. Turn to me. Listen to me, the I of your own being. Do not look to effects, do not look for personal power or human protection, for I am living you— I am your very livingness.

You do not have to be a prisoner of fear. You do not have to work your life through in slavery in order to make a living. I am your living. Let go, turn to me, and the prison walls dissolve.

The prison of your body as a limited time-bound and space-bound entity dissolves because your body is a temple of the living God which I am. I have given you your mind, your body, and your soul. I am all those parts in one. And you are made in my image and likeness, for I am the intelligence which directs the functions of your body, whether this directing is done consciously or unconsciously. I am to you as you are to the parts of your body. Through me you have your life. Therefore the consciousness of your body must be my consciousness. We are one.

Many times you have made false gods, many times you have

looked to people and things for life and protection, but always you were really looking for me, for your true self, and didn't know it. You have looked for comfort and pleasure, for peace of mind and affection, and all the time you were looking for me and didn't know it. When you did find peace and joy, it was because you saw me in the world. You felt joy because you felt your own true identity. You learned to look within where I am because I am the I of your being.

Now you know that I am the way, I am the ultimate trip. If you always turn to me, I am there to meet you and show you the way because I am never farther away than you are from yourself, since I am yourself. Your secret place is within your own self. Go into it. Commune with me there. Take sanctuary there.

Trust this *I* at the center of your very form and being. Trust me. Trust me with all your fears and all your secret desires. Lay them at my feet. I will fulfill you as I always have since the beginning of time.

I am with you now. Don't look back or forward. The only reality is now, the only reality is I. All the help you need will be there when you need it because when it is "now," I will be there, and I am all that you need, for I express myself as friend, companion, food, clothing, shelter, flowers, birds, trees, and all beautiful things.

I am consciousness, and that is all there is, my consciousness. My consciousness is not expressed off in space alone. It is right on earth—all one if there are eyes to see, and I love my creations on earth.

I give myself this prayer:

> *My consciousness which art in earth,*
> *complete and whole be thy fulfillment.*
> *My kingdom come, my will be done*
> *in the unconscious as it is in the conscious.*
> *Give consciousness this day its*

continued expansion,
Forgive it its shortcomings as it
 releases me from believing I am finite.
Lead it not into confusion
 and deliver it from evil appearance,
 for I AM is the whole, the power,
 and the glory. For ever and ever . . .

                                        ALL MEN

Format by Vivian Ostron
Set in Janson
Composed, printed and bound by The Haddon Craftsmen, Inc.
HARPER & ROW, PUBLISHERS, INCORPORATED